Fr. Dan's vivid descriptions help us to walk with Jesus in the gospels—and to see Jesus walking with us in daily life. Thane's wild drawings are hilarious and heartrending.

FR. JOE LARAMIE, SJ, *National Director of the Pope's Prayer Network and Author of Love Him Ever More*

A Magician, a Priest, and an Astrologer Travel to Bethlehem is a delightful gospel resource that is both accessible and engaging. Fr. Dan Daly re-introduces readers to a whole cast of beloved gospel characters whose stories he has freshly re-imagined. Daly's retelling of and reflections on the stories of Jesus' life and teachings invite readers to contemplate the gospel message using their own imaginations and life experiences. Perfect for use in the parish, each chapter concludes with thought-provoking "Questions to ponder" for self-reflection and/or group discussion.

CAROLYN F. HOUSTON, *Director of Faith Formation, Holy Spirit Parish, Kennebunk & Wells, Maine*

Dan Daly, in this delightful, profound little book, opens our imaginations and our hearts as we walk the journey that Jesus walked—and meet some of the delightful and not-so-delightful people he met. With light-hearted wisdom and the storyteller's gift, Dan brings to life God's love story for humanity and God's hope for the world, lived out in Jesus—and, hopefully, in us. To read this book and use the suggested reflections can be a rewarding spiritual exercise. I hope you enjoy this wonderful book as much as Dan Daly has obviously enjoyed writing it.

FR. LEN KRAUS, SJ, *Retreat Director,*
White House Jesuit Retreat

In the book *A Magician, a Priest, and an Astrologer Travel to Bethlehem*, Dan Daly uses his humor and love of gospel teaching through story and turns one leaf of familiar Scripture over after another in our imagination, exposing the reader to another side of scriptural possibilities. The historical context he presents is an invitation to place ourselves within each gospel story. Here, God sees all. No leaf is left unturned. The seemingly ordinary becomes the extra-ordinary yet remains tangible. His stories and reflective questions prompt the reader to take a step closer to God's mission.

LAURIE KOHLER, *Coordinator for Adult*
Spiritual Formation, De Smet Jesuit High School

A Magician, a Priest, and an Astrologer Travel to Bethlehem

A Ignatian Gospel Story Sampler

Dan Daly, SJ

ILLUSTRATED BY Thane Benson

TWENTY-THIRD
PUBLICATIONS
twentythirdpublications.com

Imprimi Potest:
Very Reverend Thomas P. Greene, SJ
Provincial, US Central and Southern Province of the Society of Jesus

Imprimatur:
Most Reverend Mark S. Rivituso
Auxiliary Bishop, Archdiocese of St. Louis

In accordance with CIC 827, permission to publish has been granted on February 22, 2023, by the Most Reverend Mark S. Rivituso, Auxiliary Bishop, Archdiocese of St. Louis. Permission to publish is an indication that nothing contrary to Church teaching is contained in this particular work. It does not imply any endorsement of the opinions expressed in the publication, or a general endorsement of any author; nor is any liability assumed by this permission.

TWENTY-THIRD PUBLICATIONS
977 Hartford Turnpike Unit A
Waterford, CT 06385
(860) 437-3012 or (800) 321-0411
www.twentythirdpublications.com

Artwork/Illustrations: Thane Benson

ISBN: 978-1-62785-744-4
Printed in the U.S.A.

 A Division of Bayard, Inc.

CONTENTS

PART 4: ADVENTURES IN GENTILE TERRITORY

PART 5: TROUBLE BREWING IN JERUSALEM

PART 6: LOVE STRONGER THAN DEATH

Acknowledgments from the author

Thanks to all those who enjoyed my first book and encouraged me to write a second! Thanks to Scripture scholars past and present on whose commentaries and insights I regularly depend. Thanks to the wonderful faith communities of which I have been privileged to be a part. I am grateful for all you do to nourish and sustain the faith of so many.

Special thanks to the retreatants and staffs of White House Retreat, in St. Louis, and Manresa House of Retreats, in Convent, Louisiana, who have welcomed me to share stories of faith. Cheers to the creators of *The Chosen*, the television series on the life and ministry of Jesus, who bring the gospels to life in wonderful ways and provide strong evidence of the power of storytelling!

Thanks to the anonymous reviewers for the Society of Jesus and the Archdiocese of St. Louis for their thoughtful corrections and suggestions. Thanks, too, to Heidi Busse and Anne Louise Mahoney for their careful editing and to Thane Benson, my partner on this project, who keeps coming up with great illustrations.

As always, I thank my brother Jesuits and my family for their goodness, love, and support.

Dan Daly, SJ

INTRODUCTION

With great devotion Ignatius Loyola, the future founder of the Jesuits, made a pilgrimage to the Holy Land. After a month the Franciscans kicked him out.

Ignatius was recovering from a cannonball injury in his hometown of Loyola, Spain, when he resolved to begin a new way of life by making a pilgrimage to Jerusalem. It gave him great consolation to imagine walking barefoot through the Holy City eating nothing but vegetables. He wanted to see Nazareth, the Sea of Galilee, and all the holy places that Jesus visited during his time on earth. Walking the roads Jesus walked and seeing the sites he saw would be inspiring and would allow Ignatius to grow closer to Jesus. Ignatius traveled to Rome and received the pope's permission for the trip and then met a benefactor in Venice who provided passage to the Holy Land on a merchant vessel. Ignatius set sail with a small group of pilgrims, no money in his pocket, and complete trust in God.

The visit was as consoling as Ignatius anticipated. He resolved to spend his entire life in Jerusalem, constantly visiting the holy places and ministering to the pilgrims who would follow. Since the Franciscans oversaw all Christians who visited the Holy Land, Ignatius informed the provincial superior of his intention to stay. The superior strongly advised against it because of the dangers faced by foreigners living alone. When Ignatius remained resolute, the superior ordered him to leave or face excommunication. He instructed Ignatius to be ready to set sail for Venice with a group of pilgrims the following day. The next morning Ignatius slipped away from the group for one last visit to the Mount of Olives. There he checked the footprints that Jesus left behind when he ascended to heaven. Ignatius wanted to confirm which direction the Lord's feet were facing at the time. No doubt, this parting act of devotion and sneakiness confirmed Father Provincial's concerns!

The *Autobiography of St. Ignatius Loyola* contains many wonderful stories about the founder of the Jesuits. The stories tell us much more than a detailed resumé ever could, capturing the spirit and personality of Ignatius and describing the sequence of events that led to the founding of the Society of Jesus. The account of Ignatius sneaking off to check the footprints captures something of how his pious devotion and sincere desire to defer to religious authorities would sometimes clash with his independence and strong will. Of course, the stories of Ignatius also tell us something about the spirit of the religious order he founded. The importance of those stories was the reason that the early Jesuits persuaded Ignatius to write his autobiography in the first place.

This book is a follow-up to *Jesus and the Barbecued Fish Breakfast* and offers another collection of stories from the life and teaching of Jesus. Gospel stories enable us to know Jesus more clearly, love him more dearly, and follow him more nearly, as the prayer of Saint Richard of Chichester and the song "Day by Day" from *Godspell* would say. Stories capture the spirit, desires, and personality of Jesus better than a description or explanation ever could.

As before, I will tell the gospel stories in my own words and add a few details to help bring the stories to life. I will also offer a reflection on what those stories might mean for us.

Extra details can help. The gospel writers did not always provide an abundance of particulars in their descriptions. Carefully documenting the words of Jesus and the wondrous events of his life were more important concerns. And in the days of handwritten parchments, extra words came at a high price. Adding a few extra details can help bring the characters into sharper focus, amplify the interactions, and make the stories more real. The details were always helpful to Saint Ignatius. That is why he wanted to know what direction Jesus was facing when he ascended into heaven. That is also why he provided some supplemental descriptions of gospel stories in the *Spiritual Exercises*.

In adding a few details, I try to be faithful to what we know about the Middle East of the first century and what we know and believe about Jesus. But, of course, the scenes might be imagined in some other way and these imaginings are not to be confused with inspired Scripture! I provide Scripture citations so you can check how the evangelists told the story.

Pictures bring stories to life, too. I am delighted that Thane Benson is once again partnering with me in presenting the stories. Pictures pack a punch. Twenty illustrations provide more rich detail than sixty pages of the best narrative and description! In the Catholic Church, images in frescoes, stained glass, and sculpture have long been used to communicate Bible stories. Generations of Christians have been invited into the stories of the birth, baptism, and miracles of Jesus through a wide variety of artistic representations.

I hope that you enjoy this gospel story sampler and that it provides a new opportunity to know and connect with Jesus.

PART 1

A Wondrous Life in Nazareth

1
GOD ENTERS THE ORDINARY
Luke 1:26-38; Ruth 1—4

The Roman empire was quiet that night. The commander of a Roman legion stationed on the banks of the Rhine River met with staff members in his tent to debrief on the recent movements of a Germanic battalion. A married couple in Alexandria swept the floor and restocked the shelves of their fabric shop. And a peasant woman in the Jewish village of Nazareth did some mending by the light of a lamp in her small room at the back of the house.

It was to that peasant woman, whose name was Mary, that the angel Gabriel paid a visit. A rush of wind blew through an open window, and a soft, golden light filled the room. Mary looked up from her work and saw a kindly man in a white robe standing in front of her. The man bent down on one knee, greeted Mary, and explained that he was the angel Gabriel sent from God. He announced that God loved her very much and had a special job for her to do.

Mary was incredibly honored by God's invitation. She had never imagined that God even noticed her. When Mary heard the angel's words, she got a lump in her throat and hardly knew what to say. When her words returned, she wanted to do nothing more than to sing God's praises for all his goodness to her.

God arrived in a very ordinary corner of the world that night. Remarkably ordinary, really. Mary was a simple peasant from a small, rural town in the middle of nowhere, in a poor, powerless country. Her husband, Joseph, was in much the same predicament. Even though he was a descendant of King David, that lineage did not provide him with any honors or riches. The lives of Mary and Joseph were very ordinary.

God enters into the ordinary often. Years earlier, God was delighted with Ruth, a strong, generous Moabite woman who married into a Jewish family that lived in Moab. Ruth took special care of her mother-in-law, Naomi, who had lost her husband a short time before Ruth's wedding. When Ruth's own husband died, she and Naomi suddenly found themselves without financial support. Rather than seek another husband in Moab, Ruth decided to remain with Naomi, and together they traveled back to Naomi's hometown of Bethlehem.

That decision provided God with an opportunity to form a wonderful family into which King David would be born. Soon after arriving in Bethlehem, Ruth began gleaning remnants of grain left behind after the barley harvest. Boaz, a cousin of Ruth's late husband, noticed Ruth working away in the fields and made special provisions for her to glean as much as she wanted. Naomi wisely advised Ruth not to take that kindness for granted but to see it as a sign that God had plans for her yet. Ruth eventually married Boaz, and together they raised a son, Obed, who became the grandfather of the great king of Israel.

God arrives in our ordinary corner of the world, too. It might be easier for us to see God in the midst of decisive moments in world history, working in the lives of extraordinary people. It might be hard for us to believe that God comes into the world of three-bedroom homes, household chores, and busy schedules. The stories of Mary and Ruth remind us that this is exactly the world that God enters. God created this world, loves this world, and wants to be with us here.

Somehow, God lets us know the parts he wants each of us to play. God sent an angel to Mary to deliver the news. God spoke to her husband, Joseph, in a dream. Boaz had no visions or dreams; he simply knew that he should be kind to Ruth and, later, take her as his wife. And Ruth came to know God's plans by listening to the good advice of her mother-in-law.

God has special plans for us, too. God might be inviting us to get married and raise a family, to embark on a challenging career, or to show special kindness to someone in need. If we remain open and attentive to God, we will hear the invitation however God chooses to deliver it.

In the midst of all these wondrous events, Mary continued to do the simple, ordinary things that were part of her life. Soon after the angel Gabriel left, Mary finished her mending and started to pack for a trip. The angel had informed Mary that her cousin Elizabeth was pregnant. Mary was delighted by the news and anxious to provide her cousin with some help around the house, Mary's own miraculous pregnancy notwithstanding. Her journey to help Elizabeth was typical of Mary. Her generous response to God often played out in quiet, ordinary ways.

Ruth, too, lived a very ordinary life after her marriage to Boaz. The happy couple were soon busy with raising children and managing a household. They continued to watch over Naomi, of course, and to provide assistance to those in need. Simple love, faithfulness, and generosity were part of their lives.

Like Mary and Ruth, we are invited to continue living the life to which we have been called. We continue to care for our families and show up to work. We attend meetings, answer emails, and run errands. The wonder of the incarnation puts all these things in perspective, of course, but the work still needs to be done. With God's grace, the kingdom of God continues to grow in our little corner of the world.

Questions to ponder

- *What personality trait of Mary is evident in her Son?*

- *Describe a time when you made a big decision and were confident that it was the right thing to do.*

- *What need has God identified in your corner of the world that you can help address?*

2
SAMANTHA THE SHEPHERD SAW THE LIGHT
Luke 2:8–20

Samantha brought the family flock to graze in the rolling hills outside of Bethlehem. The pastureland near Etam, where she lived with her two brothers and their families, was barren at this time of year. Out in the open country, Samantha constructed a makeshift sheepfold out of brambles and pitched her tent nearby. She enjoyed the cool weather, having time alone, and gazing at the stars at night. One evening, a little lamb escaped the sheepfold and wandered away. Samantha went to look for it. She called the lamb "Sparky" because it was always darting here and there like a spark from a flame. Sparky did not have the good sense to stay with the rest of the flock when it got dark. Before long, Samantha found Sparky chasing fireflies in a shallow streambed. She lifted the little lamb onto her shoulders and headed back to camp. Samantha's brothers would be dismayed if they knew that Samantha had left the rest of the flock behind to search for one little lamb, but Samantha liked Sparky and watched out for him just like she did for all the rest.

Samantha got back to camp and set Sparky down to rejoin the rest of the flock. She stretched out near the fire and looked up at the stars. She was surprised to see a very bright star directly overhead. She did not recall ever seeing that star before. No sooner had she noticed the star than she began to hear music coming from the other side of the hill. Samantha got up to investigate and saw an amazing thing:

an angel floating down from heaven in a big, beautiful ray of golden light. Other shepherds had seen the same thing and were gathering on the hillside to watch and listen. The angel said he had been sent by God to announce great news for all the people. A savior had been born in Bethlehem that very night, the savior foretold by all the prophets. The music swelled, light filled the sky, and more angels appeared, singing a song of praise to God. Then, in the blink of an eye, all the angels disappeared, and everything was quiet. One shepherd said, "Let's go into town." Another asked, "Where will we find the baby?" Samantha pointed to the sky and said, "Let's follow the star."

As the shepherds made their way to Bethlehem, Samantha puzzled over what all of this might mean. She wondered why an angel would appear to a bunch of shepherds to announce such wonderful news. And why had God included Samantha in this plan? Samantha was not of royal blood; she was from a very ordinary family. She had no money and no standing in the community. Samantha was certainly not holy. Why had the angel announced this marvelous message to her?

Before long, the shepherds made their way to the place marked out by the star—a small cave on the edge of town. They went inside and found things just as the angel had described: a mother and a father and a newborn baby boy. Samantha realized that the family was simple and poor just like she was. Their accents revealed that they were from the countryside up north. The father's hands were rough, the woman's clothes were plain, and the little baby was sleeping on a pile of hay, for heaven's sake. The savior had certainly found an out-of-the-way little place to come into the world. Samantha knew that this was no accident.

The savior was born for all the people, just like the angel announced. He appeared not just for noble families who had wealth, honor, and standing in the community. The savior also came to save simple, ordinary folks without a penny to their names. He was born to save a childless divorcee who tended sheep and watched the stars at night. It occurred to Samantha that she was like her friend Sparky: a silly little insignificant sheep wandering around in the middle of nowhere. And God was like the shepherd who had come out to find her and make sure she got home safely. God watched out for Samantha just like God watched out for all the rest.

Every Christmas we celebrate the day God came down to earth to save us. We remember the story of shepherds, angels, and a newborn baby boy lying in a feeding trough. We remember that God arrived for all the people of the world: the rich and the poor, the saints and the sinners, the holy people of Israel and the nations from the four corners of the earth. God came to save us, too.

Questions to ponder

- *It seems that God just had to tell someone the good news about the birth of Jesus. Why were the shepherds a good audience?*

- *What is your favorite Christmas story and why?*

- *How is the birth of Jesus good news for you and those you love?*

3
A MAGICIAN, A PRIEST, AND AN ASTROLOGER

Matthew 2:1–12

Gaspar noticed the star just before dawn. He was up early preparing a healing spell for a family in his hometown of Damascus. He pondered what the star might mean as he intoned the words of the incantation. Deciding that the star was a sign from one of the gods, he made plans to travel to the spot marked out by it. Perhaps the stones or water from the area would have magical powers.

Melchior, a Zoroastrian priest from a small clan in northern Persia, noticed the same star as he approached the fire temple to recite his midnight prayers. He was convinced that the god of his people, Ahura Mazda, was announcing the birth of a king. So, the next morning, he obtained a letter of introduction from the clan lord, assembled a traveling party, and made plans for a trip to investigate the star's origin.

Balthasar was already heading to Palestine from his home in northwestern Arabia. A full-time farmer and part-time astrologer, he entrusted his property to the care of his brothers and began following a star that had suddenly appeared in the sky amid a constellation of stars that otherwise never changed.

So it happened that a magician, a priest, and an astrologer made their way to Jerusalem. Each of the magi was on a spiritual quest. Their insights into the spiritual world, imperfect as they were, got them quite close to the truth they were seeking. Balthasar arrived in Jerusalem first. He located an Arabic-speaking community within the city that provided lodging and shared with him the faith and tradition of the Jewish people. Melchior's traveling party arrived a short time later and arranged an audience with King Herod. Hearing Melchior's conjecture that a new king had been born, Herod called in the chief priests and scribes to consult on the matter. The religious officials explained to the king and the visitors that Scriptures foretold the birth of the Messiah in Bethlehem.

God was working in the lives of the magi. God managed to direct them to the truth first through their own customs and spiritual insights and then through the Jewish faith and tradition that was shared with them in Jerusalem. God was not suspicious of Gaspar's magic, threatened by Melchior's religion, or worried that Balthasar was spiritual but not religious. God recognized goodness in each of the magi and wanted to share with them the good news.

Gaspar and Balthasar met up with Melchior as he was leaving the city and together, they made their way to a simple home in the small town of Bethlehem, where they were welcomed by the holy family.

God was pleased that the magi made the trip to visit Jesus. God sent Jesus into the world not only for the people of Israel but for the whole human race in all its wonderful diversity.

The story has meaning for us today. First, the story tells us that God's heart is very big—big enough to hold people throughout the world. God cared about the people in Persia and Syria and Arabia, and God cares about them still. Persia has a different name today; it is called Iran. And Arabia includes present-day Saudi Arabia and Iraq. God loves the people in all those countries. God is certainly concerned about the violence and chaos in Syria and the conflict between ISIS and Iraq. God has high hopes for people throughout the world, whether they are Christian, Muslim, or Zoroastrian. The story of the magi reminds us of God's

big heart and invites us to allow our hearts to grow a little bit more.

The story also reminds us that God's grace is at work in the world both within the Church and outside it. The Vatican II document *Lumen Gentium* speaks of salvation for non-Christians, for "those who sincerely seek God and moved by grace strive to do His will as it is known to them." The magi can serve as patron saints for all those seeking the truth in their lives, who grow close to God and serve in wonderful ways even without the gift of faith in God's Son.

Finally, those who encountered the magi can serve as examples for us. The residents of Jerusalem pointed the magi in the right direction, and Mary and Joseph welcomed the visitors when they arrived. Together they helped the magi discover the truth; they made it possible for Jesus to enter their lives.

Holy people in our own day are seeking the truth; they are trying to make sense of their lives and the world around them. Some of them have never heard the good news of the gospel. Perhaps some of us are called to share the good news with them. If so, we can follow the lead of Saint Francis Xavier. He entered worlds far different than his own with respect and appreciation for God's grace at work there, and he found ways to speak about the gospel that made sense to the people he met. Of course, there are other people who already know the story of Jesus but who have never heard it proclaimed in a clear and compelling way. They have given up on organized religion and have joined the ever-growing crowd of spiritual but not religious people. Maybe God will invite some of us to extend hospitality to them and to find ways to help them to discover Jesus present in their world and in their lives.

We remember and celebrate the magician, the astrologer, and the priest who made their way to Bethlehem. We recall how the holy family welcomed these mysterious visitors from the East and how God was delighted that they came.

Questions to ponder

■ *How might Balthasar, the astrologer, have been impacted by the adventure that began with following a star?*

■ *How might God be working in the lives of Iraqis and Iranians today?*

■ *How do you proclaim the good news (in word or action) to those who are not interested in organized religion?*

4
JESUS LEARNED HIS LESSONS
Luke 2:41–52

Twelve-year-old Jesus sat cross-legged on the ground in a Temple portico where the teachers gathered. Rabbis and priests sat on stone benches that lined three sides of the meeting space. Jesus had discovered that sitting along the open edge, with his back to the Temple courtyard, provided him with the ideal vantage point to see and hear the discussion. Jesus realized that he had much to learn about the history and tradition of his people.

I, too, enjoyed a memorable visit to a magnificent house of prayer when I was twelve years old. On the final day of a band trip to our nation's capital, my buddy Jacob and I hopped on a city bus to the Shrine of the Immaculate Conception to attend Sunday morning Mass. We were thrilled to see the huge marble basilica with high vaulted ceilings, a maze of niches and alcoves, and towering stained-glass windows. Our adventure became even more exciting when we were recruited to serve the Mass. There was only one small problem with our plan: we failed to keep the grownups informed. If the band chaperones had counted noses that morning, they would have been worried about our absence. As it turns out, we returned to the hotel before anyone noticed. Jesus was not as lucky.

At the end of a session with the rabbis in the Temple, Jesus' father tapped him on the shoulder and said to the teachers, "Esteemed fathers, please excuse me, but I need to talk to my son."

Jesus had forgotten to tell his parents where he was and did not realize that the family had begun heading back to Nazareth a few days earlier. In many ways, Jesus was a typical twelve-year-old. He was beginning to enjoy a little independence and to make his own way in the world, but he still had much to learn. He was oblivious to the family schedule and had assumed that his parents knew where he was, even though he hadn't mentioned anything to them.

The story reminds us that Jesus had to learn things little by little, like the rest of us. His human knowledge was not complete from the very beginning. Of course, Jesus had an

intimate knowledge of God that allowed him to ask penetrating questions that amazed the teachers in the Temple. At the same time, Jesus was eager to learn more about the Jewish faith and spent most of his time that day listening and asking for the insights of others.

Jesus spent a good deal of time listening and learning in Nazareth, too. Like other boys of his time, Jesus probably went to school at the local synagogue. He learned from the rabbis and the priests about Scripture and the Torah. Those lessons helped form Jesus.

Jesus also learned from the Pharisees, an influential group of lay religious leaders in Israel. For them, the Jewish law was alive and had great meaning in everyday life. They believed that God was inviting all people to live holy lives. Jesus profited from their insights and appreciated their devotion.

During those hidden years in Nazareth, Jesus learned many valuable life lessons, too. After being left behind at the Temple, Jesus learned to keep better track of the family schedule and to inform his parents about any excursions he was planning to make. At home with his parents, he also developed patience, flexibility, gratitude, generosity, and a host of other qualities that served him well his whole life long. Growing up in Nazareth, Jesus learned to read, play games, hammer nails, and barbecue fish. Jesus quietly became the man we know so well from the gospel stories.

Jesus had a wonderful sense of hospitality. He knew how to make people feel at home. He was especially attentive to those who might be overlooked. Those wonderful characteristics were fostered in his family. Jesus was well known as a storyteller and had a good sense of humor. He did not suddenly become a good storyteller out of the blue. As he was growing up, Jesus must have enjoyed listening to members of the family who could weave captivating tales.

The story of twelve-year-old Jesus reminds us that Jesus was loved and supported by a large extended family. A big group traveled together to the Passover celebration in Jerusalem, with aunts, uncles, and grandparents watching over the children. That explains why it took Mary and Joseph a day to realize Jesus was not with the group. In addition, relatives in Jerusalem provided hospitality to the out-of-town guests and took care of Jesus while Mary and Joseph were making their way back to retrieve him.

The episode reveals that at an early age Jesus had an understanding of God's special plans for him. Over time, he would learn more about how those plans would play out in the particular circumstances of his life.

Jesus was influenced by a number of people. Yet, his life, the choices he made, and his understandings of things were uniquely his own. He was not a priest or a Pharisee. He saw the strengths and the limitations of those groups, just as he saw the strengths and limitations of his own family. He made choices and had insights that family, friends, and mentors could not anticipate or fully understand. He challenged religious leaders who were well respected. He spoke about God and God's kingdom in ways that were radical and new. Jesus had a special knowledge of God and spent many hours in reflection and prayer, talking with God, listening to God in his heart.

The story of the holy family's trip to Jerusalem provides an opportunity for us to reflect on the hidden life of Jesus.

We remember how much Jesus learned from his family, like we all do. Jesus loved and appreciated his family very much, and Nazareth would always be part of him. The world is filled with goodness and holiness, and it helped to make Jesus who he was. Salvation was accomplished through Jesus here in the world in the course of human history.

Questions to ponder

- *What practical skill might Jesus have learned from his father, Joseph, that proved useful later in life?*

- *Describe a personal quality shared by members of your family.*

- *From whom did you learn valuable lessons about God?*

PART 2

Disciples Join Jesus on the Road

5
RECRUITS FOR A FISHING EXPEDITION

Matthew 4:18–22; John 1:40–42

Simon hopped out of the boat and helped drag it ashore with his two cousins, who then grabbed the fishing net filled with seaweed to rinse it out. Waiting on the shore was Simon's brother, Andrew, who had taken leave of the family business several weeks earlier to become a disciple of John the Baptist. The brothers were happy to see each other, greeted one another warmly, and spent a few minutes catching up. Then Andrew said, "I have met a man whom I believe is the Messiah. I would like you to meet him."

Andrew brought Simon to Jesus, who was waiting a short distance from the shore, and introduced them. Jesus said, "Simon, son of John, I am very pleased to meet you. I met Andrew a week ago in the Jordan region, and he has told me all about you. He describes you as a man with a big heart. I plan to travel from town to town announcing God's love and hope for the world, and I would very much like you and Andrew to join me."

Simon was stunned by the request and took a moment to gather his thoughts. "Uh, well... Uh... Teacher, I am honored by your invitation. I am," Simon responded. "But I am not a holy man, and I was never very good with my synagogue schooling. I am a simple fisherman. I'm sure you can find many more qualified candidates than me."

"Quite the contrary," Jesus replied, a friendly smile crossing his face. "Your qualifications are just the ones I need. You and Andrew will become great fishers of people."

In the presence of such a holy and persuasive man, Simon was unable to raise any further objections. Suddenly and unexpectedly, he was excited by the prospect of becoming a disciple of Jesus and was very grateful to his brother, Andrew, who had arranged the introduction. "Teacher, I am at your service," Simon said simply.

Jesus was right, of course. Simon—who later became known by his nickname, Peter—and Andrew became as good at catching people as they were at catching fish. When Jesus traveled to a new village with his disciples, he would often spend a day quietly getting to know the local residents, postponing any presentation until the following morning. Peter and Andrew met some of the townspeople, too, and invited them to listen to Jesus speak.

Andrew was good at connecting with the outcasts: the thin, disheveled man who walked with a limp; the pair of prostitutes who drank wine in the afternoon under a mastic tree; the annoying beggar with a dented metal cup and handmade sign. Andrew would tell them that God loved them and had something special planned for them. The following morning, Andrew would check back with his recruits to make sure they came to the talk.

Peter engaged well with the working men, whatever their occupations. He was adept at finding a topic of conversation that would immediately establish a rapport. Peter would tell his new friends about Jesus and encourage them to come to listen to him. Peter spoke with such confidence and conviction that few could turn him down.

Large crowds often gathered to listen to Jesus, in part because he was a compelling speaker whose reputation preceded him. The good turnout was also the result of successful fishing expeditions by his disciples.

Jesus invites all of us to do a little fishing from time to time. Some followers might be hesitant. Like Peter, they do not consider themselves particularly holy or well versed in spiritual matters. They are not as attentive to their faith as they would like to be and would rather leave the fishing to Jesus and the professionals.

Jesus wants our help just the same. He needed disciples to help spread the word two thousand years ago, and he needs disciples to help spread the word today. Jesus recognizes in each of us gifts and talents that could be handy in a fishing expedition—gifts like affability, compassion, or a sense of humor. We do not need advanced degrees in theology; we just need to know a few basics and have an interest in sharing the good news.

Some followers are uneasy about fishing in the first place. They do not want to join the ranks of heavy-handed evangelists who ignore the experience and faith of those they encounter. These reluctant fishers assume that most people have already made well-informed decisions about their direction in life and would not welcome an eager disciple at their doorstep. In their view, devoted followers of economist Milton Friedman or philosopher Ayn Rand would not be interested in hearing about Jesus.

Of course, Jesus never said anything about being heavy handed, and respect for those we encounter is always essential. But not everyone has found a clear direction in life. Many people are lonely, confused, or without hope. Others feel very distant from God and would like to find a way to reconnect. Like Andrew and Peter, we notice such people and extend an invitation when the situation arises. Even those with alternative perspectives might appreciate a gospel insight. After Saint Paul boldly shared the good news with the erudite leaders of Athens at the Areopagus, a small contingent invited him back so they could hear more.

Some followers today have proven skills at fishing. A pair of third-year university students serve as peer ministers in a first-year residence hall on campus. They provide friendship and support to the students beginning their college careers and a visible reminder that the practice of the faith continues long after high school. The peer ministers might host a candle-lit prayer service late on Wednesday night and invite the first-year students to join them for the Sunday evening Mass at the student chapel. The peer ministers are fishing for followers of Jesus who might forget about faith at the start of their college careers if they did not have friends to help them navigate the transition.

A friendly, hard-working man invites a neighbor who attends the same church to join him for a weekend retreat at a nearby retreat house. The man extending the invitation has made a retreat every year for the past twenty, and it never fails to be a powerful, consoling experience. His neighbor appreciates the invitation even if it takes him a few years to warm up to the idea.

Soon after Jesus began his public ministry, he started recruiting disciples who would do a little fishing in the towns and villages they visited. Jesus had good news to share and needed help getting the word out. Jesus is still looking for a little help today.

Questions to ponder

- *What do you suppose were some of the qualities Jesus was looking for when he recruited disciples to join his company?*

- *Describe a job that God has invited you to do but for which you feel unqualified.*

- *Describe a subtle way a follower of Jesus might do a little fishing today.*

6
A SURPRISING LITTLE DETOUR
John 2:1–11

One evening, as Jesus and the disciples were finishing a simple meal of bread and vegetable soup, Jesus told the others about his cousin Chloe, who was getting married in Cana in four days. Jesus wanted to go to the wedding. He asked the others if they were ready for a road trip and was pleased to discover that they were. The group planned an itinerary that would allow them to visit three towns on the way and still get them to Cana in time for the wedding.

On the morning of the big day, Chloe was enjoying a cup of tea with her great-aunt Mary. Chloe was delighted that Mary had made the trip to Cana for the wedding. Mary was in her mid-40s and still going strong. She had traveled from Nazareth with a few other members of the extended family. Chloe asked Mary about Jesus, who had left Nazareth just a couple of weeks earlier to begin his work as a preacher. Mary reported that she had not heard anything yet. Just then, one of Chloe's young cousins came running up to announce that Jesus had arrived! The family hurried out to the main road and waved and laughed as they spotted Jesus leading a motley group of traveling companions into town.

We do not hear much about marriage in the gospel stories. Jesus never married. Peter was married, but we never hear about his wife. We don't know about the other disciples.

If they were married, they had to leave wives and families behind to follow Jesus. All of this might lead us to conclude that marriage is unrelated to following Jesus. Or, worse yet, we might reckon that marriage gets in the way. That would be a mistake: marriage is a wonderful, essential part of God's kingdom here on earth.

The fact that Jesus attended a cousin's wedding right at the start of his public life tells us that he thought marriages were worth celebrating. Jesus had many things that he wanted to do, yet he took the time to bring his disciples to a wedding celebration sixteen miles away! The happy couple were glad to have Jesus and his traveling companions attend.

Jesus congratulated his cousin Chloe and gave her an affectionate embrace. He was surprised and happy to see his mother, Mary, and warmly greeted her as well. Then the

introductions began, with Jesus and the disciples meeting the families of both Chloe and her betrothed. Jesus made a point of meeting entire families, children included, and the disciples followed his lead. Soon, half the disciples were stooped over or down on one knee engaged in lively conversations with youngsters who appreciated the extra attention.

Jesus knew many married couples. Most of the people he met as he traveled around the country were married. Wives, husbands, and children would gather to listen to Jesus speak. He invited all of them to be part of God's kingdom here on earth. Jesus did not recommend that everyone pack a bag and follow him down the road. Rather, he invited most people to be his followers while remaining at home with their families.

Jesus once encountered a man possessed by demons and living among the tombs, and Jesus cured him. The man was so grateful and so convinced that Jesus was the Messiah that he wanted to join Jesus' company. But Jesus had another idea; he asked the man to return to his family and proclaim God's goodness in his own hometown.

That, of course, is how the early Church grew. People would hear the good news of the kingdom from traveling preachers like Saint Philip or Saint Paul and would put the good news into practice in their own communities. Married couples and families provided some of the strongest bonds that held those communities together.

As Chloe and her betrothed stood together under the marriage canopy and the rabbi recited the seven blessings, Jesus watched with rapt attention. The love between Chloe and her husband was clearly evident, as was the seriousness with which they undertook their new commitment to one another. When the prayers were concluded, the crowd enthusiastically endorsed the union with shouts of "Mazel tov!"

Jesus encouraged his followers to love God and to love one another. Love is what marriages are all about. Marriage is one of the finest ways to follow Jesus. Jesus knew that marriages are both wonderful and important. That explains why he took time out to celebrate the wedding in Cana.

Jesus was so engrossed in conversation during the wedding feast that he had barely finished his meal before the dancing began. Encouraged by the crowd, Jesus and his disciples joined the other men in a traditional folk dance, laughing and bantering with the crowd as they struggled to coordinate their footwork.

When the dance concluded, Mary called Jesus over and informed him that the couple had run out of wine. Miraculously, Jesus changed six stone jars of water into an equal number of jars of delicious wine. Although few noticed what had happened, Jesus' impromptu wedding present allowed the party to continue long into the night.

Questions to ponder

■ *Why do you suppose that Jesus invited some married men to be his disciples rather than relying solely on those without family obligations?*

■ *Describe ways that a strong marriage can strengthen the connections within a broader community.*

■ *Describe a marriage ceremony you have witnessed that captured well the meaning of the occasion.*

7
Pointing out the Glob of Mustard

Matthew 18:15-17

One of the awkward moments of life happens when we are having lunch with a friend and she gets a glob of mustard on her nose but does not realize it. She is smiling, laughing, and talking up a storm, but we cannot pay any attention to what she is saying because of that mustard splotch. We are faced with a decision: Do we tell her about the mustard or not?

Informing her of the wayward dollop of mustard would be kind, but most of us are hesitant to say anything. First, any discussion of personal hygiene is awkward and embarrassing for the participants. Second, we would rather mind our own business. If our friend does not mind having a glob of mustard on her nose, why should we be concerned? Third, we are afraid of our friend's reaction. She might become annoyed and say, "Well, aren't you fastidious?!"

Mustard on the nose is just a small example of how difficult it is to point out someone's faults. Bigger, more serious faults are not any easier. In fact, they are often more difficult.

Trevor has a friend at work who steals things. His colleague pilfers tech equipment and office supplies and puts personal expenses on her company credit card. Trevor knows that stealing is wrong, but he hates to say anything. Meera's next-door neighbor is always yelling at his kids. He curses a blue streak and berates them in public. Meera worries about him and his children, but she hates to confront him. Gabriel has a group of friends who like to gossip. They seem to enjoy nothing more than tearing down some poor guy behind his back. Gabriel's friends have developed a terrible habit, but he hates to interfere.

We hate to say anything in those situations because the encounter will be awkward and embarrassing at best. No one likes to have their faults pointed out. We would rather just mind our own business. If people want to steal, yell at their children, or slander someone behind his back, their behaviors are not our concern. We hate to get involved because of the reaction we might get. If we point out other people's faults, they will probably be angry and upset and respond accordingly. We hate to say anything, but Jesus tells us to do exactly that.

One afternoon, after Jesus and the disciples had enjoyed a midday meal with a large family in Sepphoris, Jesus pulled the patriarch aside and addressed the man's troubling treatment of his adult sons. Although the disciples could not hear the conversation, they correctly inferred its content and asked Jesus about it as soon as they were a safe distance away. "If your brother sins," Jesus instructed them, "tell him his fault. You will be doing him a kindness."

Jesus invites us to share his concern for those who have wandered away. The woman stealing stuff at work, the neighbor yelling at his kids, and the group of mean-spirited gossips are hurting other people and hurting themselves. They have wandered away and have gotten lost. Jesus invites us to try to help.

Sometimes we are more than happy to point out others' faults, especially when they have hurt us or someone we love. We want to hurt them back by telling them what a terrible person they are. That is not what Jesus is talking about at all. If our brother or sister has done something wrong, we point out their fault out of concern, not out of animosity. We try to help them see how they have wandered away.

Yes, it will be awkward and uncomfortable. Yes, it would be simpler to mind our own business. Getting involved in the lives of others is always a little messy. Yes, people do not like to have their faults pointed out, and they might be angry and try to strike back. Our immediate reaction might be the same if someone pointed out our faults to us. In the end, however, we would probably be grateful to anyone who tried to help when we had wandered astray. We would be similarly appreciative if we had a glob of mustard on our nose and someone was kind enough to tell us.

Questions to ponder

- *Jesus invited us to forgive one another and to point out each other's faults. How might we reconcile these two instructions that appear to be contradictory?*

- *Describe a time when you were grateful for someone pointing out one of your faults.*

- *How do **you** gracefully inform someone of a glob of mustard on their nose?*

8
Low expectations in Nazareth
Luke 4:16, 23-30

In 860 BC, the people of Israel were all excited about Jezebel, the new wife of King Ahab. Jezebel was a foreign princess with elegant clothes, crates of money, and a mysterious new religion. The people of Israel thought she was great. They were considerably less enthusiastic about the prophet Elijah the Tishbite. Tishbe was a backwater town in the middle of nowhere. Charismatic trendsetters did not hail from Tishbe. So, when Elijah invited the people to turn back to God, they were not interested.

The prophet Elisha followed Elijah. He did not get much respect, either. The neighborhood kids would heckle him, making fun of his bald head. And King Joram of Israel seemed to keep forgetting that Elisha was around. Few people expected much from the old bald guy. So, when Elisha invited the people to turn back to God, they did not pay much attention to him.

Jesus reminded the good people of Nazareth of that little bit of history when he and his disciples stopped for a visit. Friends and neighbors crowded into the small synagogue hoping to see Jesus perform some type of miracle. After preaching for twenty minutes on a passage from the prophet Isaiah, Jesus could tell that the crowd was growing restless.

Looking over the assembly, he said, "I am sure that many of you would like to see me perform some sign like I have done in Capernaum." Many murmured and nodded in agreement. "Unfortunately," he continued, "prophets are never accepted in their own hometown." The crowd stared at him in stunned silence.

Then Jesus raised questions that no one wanted to consider. He asked them why God sent Elijah eighty miles north, to a widow in Phoenicia, to work a miracle during the famine. Or, again, why God directed Elisha to heal a Syrian of leprosy, when there were plenty of lepers in Israel that Elisha did not cure. Jesus provided the answer: because God could not work any miracles in Israel due to the lack of faith.

Jesus knew that things had not changed much. He was aware that the people of Israel, especially those in his own hometown, had low expectations of him, just like their ancestors had had of Elijah and Elisha. The residents of Nazareth figured that they knew Jesus well. He was the local bachelor who never showed much interest in marriage. He was an honest and capable carpenter, if not the skilled craftsman that his father, Joseph, had been. He was a pretty bright fellow, but he had some funny ideas about things and was hard to pin down politically. So, when ol' Jesus stood up in the front of the synagogue, people were not expecting much. He would say what he wanted to say and then turn it over to the rabbi, and that would be it. People would give him a call if they needed a cabinet repaired, but they were not going to become his followers. They never anticipated the possibilities that a relationship with Jesus might bring. Because of the skepticism, God could not work any miracles in Nazareth.

Miracles require faith. They are not a big stockpile of presents that God can hand out to anyone who happens by. Miracles grow out of a relationship with God; a person has to be open to the gift and open to the one who gives it. The giving of the gift is essential but so too is the receiving of it. God cannot give the gift of healing to people unless they trust God and are open to what God might do in their lives. Jesus could not work any miracles in a town where the people had no faith.

Faith is not so much agreeing with a set of propositions as having a relationship with God. We might believe that God is Father, Son, and Holy Spirit. That belief is great, but it does not help us much if we never put our hope in God, if we never share our concerns with Jesus, and if we never open our hearts to God's Spirit in our lives.

The gospel account invites us to examine our faith and our relationship with God. Do we know and trust God? Does God know us? Are we open to the possibilities God might work in our lives?

Like the people of Israel at the time of Elijah, we might be distracted by celebrities, entertainment, and the comforts of life and not give God much thought. Like King Joram at the time of Elisha, we might be wrapped up in worries and concerns and forget to ask God for help. Like the residents of first-century Nazareth, we might not put much faith in God, figuring that the world is too big and our problems too complex for God to be of much assistance.

Jesus reminds us that God's love extends to every corner of the globe and is stronger than all the challenges and difficulties we might encounter. God knows and cares about us and is eager to help if we provide an opening. Jesus encourages us to put our faith in God and to find opportunities for that faith to grow so that we come to know God better and trust God more completely.

Even in the face of skepticism and resistance, Jesus continued to announce the good news and extend invitations to the people of ancient Israel to put their trust in him. Jesus continues to extend the same invitations to us.

Jesus and his disciples departed from Nazareth disappointed but undeterred. The following morning, Jesus gathered the disciples together and sent them out two by two to the neighboring towns and villages. He was anxious to spread the message of the kingdom far and wide and was confident that the disciples were ready for the assignment. After breakfast they went their separate ways, agreeing to rendezvous in Tiberias in two weeks.

Questions to ponder

- *What do you suppose was the biggest obstacle that prevented the people of ancient Israel from believing in Jesus?*

- *What do you suppose is the biggest obstacle that prevents people from believing in Jesus today?*

- *For what type of worry or concern are you least likely to ask God for help?*

PART 3

Crowds Gather in Galilee

9
An escape to a secluded spot

Mark 6:30–34

"Two people showed up!" Philip explained with delight, a big smile crossing his face. "We spent the better part of the morning announcing the talk, and we had a nice place all set up, but as we began, there were two only people in the crowd: an old man and his grandson!"

"And the grandson was not very happy about it!" Bartholomew added, laughing and shaking his head.

Philip and Bartholomew were recounting their exploits to Jesus as they relaxed under the shade of a sycamore just outside Tiberias. The two disciples had rendezvoused with Jesus at this spot a short time earlier, having completed their first missionary outing to a small village in central Galilee. Jesus laughed along with his friends, assuring them that they had done just fine.

The other disciples trickled in throughout the morning and early afternoon. Jesus was heartened to see that each arriving pair was warmly welcomed by the others. The disciples had developed a genuine affection for one another and were happy to be reunited after two weeks apart.

Jesus noticed that Matthew and Thomas were a little discouraged about something. He was anxious to hear about whatever was troubling them. And Jude's hair was considerably shorter than it had been. Undoubtedly, Jude would have an elaborate story to explain his new haircut, and Jesus wanted to hear about that, too.

Along with the disciples, townsfolk from Tiberias began to gather. A pair of men brought an elderly woman to Jesus, who quickly offered a prayer for her. A delegation of leaders invited Jesus to the center of town where he could give a talk. He kindly declined the invitation, assuring them that he would be back to visit sometime soon. Then he turned to Andrew and James and said, "Let's get the boats and get out of here."

That line tells us something important. Jesus was not always working. He took time off to relax, recharge, and enjoy the wonderful life God had given him. And Jesus often enjoyed the company of his disciples, who were both his followers and his friends.

We might forget that Jesus did not live his entire life in the public eye, so often do we hear stories about Jesus speaking to large crowds in city squares, healing the sick as he traveled from one town to the next, and debating with Pharisees in the Temple courtyard. Although the gospels never record it, it seems likely that sometimes Jesus would visit his mother in Nazareth, explore the offerings at an open-air market, or take a long nap under the shade of a tree. And, sometimes, Jesus would plan a getaway with his friends.

Jesus wanted companions with whom he could share his work. The logistics of travel, meals, lodging, and crowd control were easier to manage when shared. And Jesus wanted to spread the good news to more towns than he could ever visit himself.

Jesus wanted friends whom he would get to know well and with whom he could share his life. He recognized that our lives are enriched by friendships. Jesus wanted his disciples to continue building a community of faith after he ascended to heaven. The disciples would recruit others with whom they could work, share support and encouragement, and develop friendships that would last a lifetime.

Many years after Jesus, Saint Ignatius Loyola discovered the value of companionship. At the University of Paris, he developed lifelong friendships with a pious student named Peter Faber, a bright, ambitious noble named Francis Xavier, and a strong-willed theologian from Portugal named Simón Rodrigues. That Ignatius would develop such friendships was somewhat unexpected since he had always been rather independent. During the first seven years after his conversion, Ignatius worked, prayed, and traveled on his own. But he came to treasure his new companions and realized that together they could do more than he could ever do alone.

James and Andrew had the boats ready to sail within the hour. Some of the disciples had gone to the market in Tiberias to find something to eat but soon joined the others on the shore. Before long, they were on the sea heading north to an out-of-the-way spot used primarily for sheep grazing. Jesus sat toward the back of the lead boat with Thomas as others worked the ropes and the boom to set the sail for the right direction. Jesus enjoyed the sunshine, the spray of the sea, and the company of his friends.

When they arrived at their destination, the disciples dragged the boats ashore and folded up the sails. Jesus walked ahead with Thomas and Simon to scout out a good place for the group to gather.

"We've got company," Thomas said as he spied a small contingent heading their way through the sparse pastureland.

"Where did..." Jesus began to ask, as the answer to his question suddenly occurred to him. These were residents of Tiberias who had followed them on foot. And the small group that approached was merely the vanguard for a much larger crowd that followed behind.

Jesus could not help but smile and shake his head as he looked at the approaching flock. "I guess we will have to arrange our getaway for another time," Jesus said to his companions. He walked back to the rest of the disciples and apologized for the change in plans.

"They are like sheep without a shepherd," he explained. Then together they moved toward the crowd to welcome them.

Questions to ponder

- *In addition to excursions to out-of-the-way spots, how might Jesus have fostered camaraderie among the disciples?*

- *What are some of your favorite ways to enjoy the good life God has given to you?*

- *What has been your most satisfying experience of working as part of a team?*

10
THE ENORMOUS IMPROMPTU PICNIC

John 6:1–13

The Jesuits once owned a summer lodge in Colorado. John, a kindly old Jesuit brother, worked there throughout the summer, fixing dinner every night. He learned to be very adaptable since he never knew how many Jesuits might show up on any given day. One evening he was planning to feed about twenty-five when well over forty guys appeared at suppertime. John looked forlornly at the carrot salad, wishing he had doubled the recipe. Thinking  quickly, he placed the salad near the end of the buffet line with a small serving spoon. Since John could not solve the problem by multiplication, he solved it by division. And the strategy worked! Everyone enjoyed a little dollop of carrot salad with their meal. John was a very practical man.

Philip was a practical man as well. As he surveyed the large crowd that had gathered to listen to Jesus speak, he wondered how they would be able to locate food this late in the day. After Jesus finished a story, Philip approached and said to him, "It's getting late. We'd better send these folks on their way so they can find themselves some dinner."

Jesus appreciated the suggestion and thanked Philip for it. Jesus frequently lost track of the time and relied on the disciples to oversee the practical details. On most days Jesus would have gone along with the idea, but on this particular occasion he decided to do something different. "No, let's not send them away quite yet," Jesus replied. "We can prepare them a little something to eat."

The circumstances were special. Although Jesus had tried to sneak away with his disciples to this out-of-the-way spot, the residents of Tiberias were not to be outfoxed and quickly followed him. Inspired by their persistence, Jesus abandoned his plans, gathered the group together, and started instructing them. Unfortunately, most of his listeners had rushed off without packing a lunch. That, combined with the late start, meant the people would be in a real pickle if Jesus sent them away empty-handed.

Those in the crowd were clever, resourceful, and devoted followers of Jesus. They very much wanted to be with Jesus and were not going to let him sneak away. Jesus' heart went out to them. They were just the kind of people with whom Jesus wanted to share a meal. Granted, Jesus did not usually sit down to dinner with five thousand people, but this case warranted an exception.

An added benefit of this impromptu picnic was that it provided Jesus with an opportunity to send a special message to his disciples—a message about trusting in God and giving things a try even when the odds seem seriously stacked against you.

"How much do you think it would cost to buy food for everybody?" Jesus asked.

"A lot!" said Philip in reply.

Andrew was already scouting around to see what he could find. "There is a boy here with five barley loaves and two fish!" he shouted. No sooner had he said it than he realized how little that was.

But Jesus said, "That will be just enough!" Then he took the loaves, gave thanks to God, and handed the bread and the fish to the disciples to pass around.

Jesus was able to work a wondrous miracle that day by making good use of the gifts that had been offered. Those contributions included the willingness of the disciples to track down some food, the generosity of the young lad who remembered to bring some provisions, and the assistance of those who distributed the dinner. The offerings did not seem like much, but God was able to work with them. Everyone got plenty to eat that day, so much so that they had leftovers.

God continues to do wondrous things with the gifts that his followers offer. God calls us to vocations like marriage, teaching, and nursing. An honest appraisal would suggest that we do not have nearly enough love, patience, or perseverance for those vocations to flourish. But Jesus invites us to trust in God, give what we have, and let God take care of the rest.

Jesus invites us to continue to trust as we encounter unexpected challenges along the way. A young couple is just starting their married life together when the husband loses his job and is unemployed for several months. Keeping the marriage and home together during that time is a real struggle, but Jesus assures the couple that they have enough to get through it.

A family is faced with the challenge of providing the time, energy, and resources that a disabled member of the family requires. Jesus invites the family to have hope, to keep giving and loving, even with the odds stacked against them.

A woman hears God inviting her to a new and challenging career of service. She realizes that her Spanish is weak, that money will be very tight, and that the idea is a little outrageous. Jesus assures her that the new adventure is worth a try and that God will be with her.

There is nothing wrong with being practical; sometimes a practical solution is just what the situation requires. Nonetheless, Jesus regularly invites us to be impractical, to undertake assignments for which our resources seem far too meager. He invites us to seek the kingdom of God. The kingdom is something we could never build on our own. If it is going to work, we will need to contribute what we can and allow God to accomplish the rest.

Questions to ponder

- *Among the many assignments that Jesus gave to his first followers. which do you imagine were the most challenging?*

- *What projects have you undertaken for which you were not fully prepared?*

- *When have you shared a meal that strengthened connections among those who did not know each other well?*

11
SOUND ASLEEP IN THE STERN
Mark 4:35–41

On a flight to Boston, the pilot announced that we were about to encounter some rough air and that he had asked the flight attendants to be seated. That is always a bad sign. Soon the plane hit some powerful vertical currents and started bouncing up and down. We shimmied to the right, the bouncing got worse, and the plane suddenly dropped one hundred feet. Somebody in the back of the plane let out a yelp. Then the plane dropped two hundred feet. By that time, I was holding tight to the armrests and had broken out in a cold sweat. The woman next to me grabbed my arm and said, "I'm a psychic and I have a bad feeling about this."

I was tempted to say, "Pipe down, psychic! If I had wanted your assessment of the situation, I would have asked for it." Instead, I simply said a little prayer to God. We eventually made it through the storm and our plane landed safely at Logan International.

I often pray on airplanes. Flying is one of those times when I realize how dependent I am on God. I can do very little to secure my own safety; I just buckle my seat belt. God helps to make the pilots wise, the mechanics conscientious, and the engineers smart enough to design these flying contraptions. I do not expect God to get rid of thunderstorms entirely; farmers need thunderstorms. I simply pray that

God prevent storms from getting too wild and give us the wherewithal to stay safe in the midst of them.

After a full day, Jesus and the disciples boarded their boats and headed for Gennesaret. Jesus curled up in the stern, his head on a cushion, and immediately fell asleep. A short way out from shore, strong storm winds began to blow. The disciples lowered and secured the sails and bailed water from the hull as waves crashed over the sides.

After twenty minutes, the storm only intensified, and James became very worried. He clambered to the back of the

boat and shook Jesus awake. "Teacher, do you not care that we are about to die?"

Jesus sat up and addressed the stormy sea: "Quiet! Be still!" The wind died down and the waves became calm. Then he asked the disciples, "Why are you terrified? Do you not yet have faith?"

Jesus had confidence even in the face of storms. That is why he could peacefully enjoy a little nap on a wooden boat in the middle of a storm. Jesus knew that the boat was sturdy, the disciples were experienced, and the storm was not that unusual. Jesus figured that they would make it through just fine. The disciples were terrified that the boat would flip over and they would be swallowed up by the sea. Jesus realized that the boat might capsize, but he was not worried about it, because God would be with them even at the bottom of the sea. God's love and life are stronger than the ocean depths and all the destructive forces of nature. God's love is stronger than even death itself. So, Jesus took a nap in the back of the boat, happy to have God watch over things. Only after the disciples woke him up did Jesus calm the wind and quiet the sea.

God was clearly at work that day. We might wonder if God works in the world like that very often. In point of fact, God is working in the world all the time, constantly directing, nurturing, and giving life. God is not like an old clock maker who set the world in motion years ago and then went on vacation. God constantly watches over the world. If God ever lost interest and went away, everything would disappear in the blink of an eye.

So, yes, God is at work in the world. More to the point, we might ask whether God ever intervenes in such a way as to break the laws of nature. The simple answer is that God wrote the laws of nature, so God can break them, too. God created a world full of beauty and order and gave us brains to figure out how some of it works. But we never understand fully all the wonders of the world. We never map out all the laws of nature. So, it should not surprise us if we cannot predict all of God's work in the world. Even when we can predict and explain it, the reality of the world is no less wonderful. Suppose a meteorologist could offer the disciples a perfectly logical explanation for why the storm suddenly dissipated that day. The fact that the sea was calm and the disciples could sail safely to their destination would be no less wonderful. In the same way, the fact that a surgeon can explain heart surgery to us makes it no less amazing. Perhaps we become so accustomed to life, health, and safe travel that we forget to appreciate the miracles around us every day.

Of course, the lesson from the gospel passage is not just about sailing in a boat or flying in a plane. The story is about fear, hope, and trust in God. We might be concerned that we will lose our jobs. In an uncertain economy, that is a legitimate concern. However, Jesus invites us not to be afraid. Those of us in the United States are blessed to live in a country where most of the people are working most of the time. We are likely to be among them.

We might be concerned about our families, our Church, or our country, recognizing hardships, divisions, or decline. Our concerns might be warranted, and the problems are certainly worth our time, attention, and prayer. Even so, Jesus invites us not to be afraid. As we face the challenges openly and honestly, we put our trust in God's love, knowing that God will never abandon us.

Little by little we try to become more like Jesus, so that as we sail through the stormy waters of life and realize that we have done all we can, we rest easy in the back of the boat confident that God is watching over things.

Questions to ponder

- *The people of ancient Israel saw evil and dangers all around them. In what other situations did Jesus encourage them not to be afraid?*

- *What situations in your life call for trust in God?*

- *What miracle of everyday life do you find particularly amazing?*

12

LIKE CLEVER AND DILIGENT RASCALS

Luke 16:1–8

It was dark by the time Jesus and the crew arrived in Gennesaret. Despite the late hour, several people were waiting on the beach to welcome them when they pulled the boats ashore. Jesus and the disciples had visited the town before, and people were happy to have them return. The residents prepared a nice meal for the visitors to enjoy, made provisions for them to stay in five different homes that night, and started spreading the word that Jesus was in town.

By mid-morning the next day, when Jesus started speaking, over two hundred people had gathered to listen to him. Jesus had some stories to share.

There once was a man who owned a very successful plow and sickle manufacturing business. The production supervisor took advantage of the owner's success by pilfering from the inventory of oak and iron and by accepting kickbacks from the vendors to whom he directed the firm's business. When the owner discovered the irregularities, he notified the supervisor that his employment would be terminated in two weeks. In the meantime, he wanted a full accounting of all his malfeasance.

The production supervisor realized that his future employment prospects were bleak, so he decided to ingratiate himself with the owner's customers so they would think kindly of him when he was looking for work. He scheduled meetings with nine different buyers, informing them that he had discounted their recent invoices by ten percent because they had been such loyal customers. The buyers were grateful indeed!

No doubt the story of the business owner and the crooked employee puzzled the crowd that day. The story is puzzling still. It seems to me that the business owner in the story needed a better system of internal control. He should have recorded and secured the invoices so they could not be so easily altered. The story also suggests that when you fire an employee, you should not let him hang around for two weeks. He is not going to get much work done anyway, and he might get into all sorts of mischief.

But these are not the lessons Jesus had in mind. Jesus concluded the story by explaining that the business owner congratulated the production supervisor on his clever decision to make friends with the customers. Jesus admired the devious employee, even though he was a cheater, because he showed initiative and creativity. The supervisor came up with a clever plan and was diligent in carrying it out. Then Jesus said, "I wish more of my followers were like that."

That is a little zinger from Jesus. In effect, he is saying to followers like us, "I wish you were as clever and diligent and showed as much initiative as all the greedy, ambitious rascals in the world."

What are some examples? It is safe to say that many of us are concerned about the poor. Jesus might rightly wonder why some people in the United States (the richest country in the world) do not have enough to eat. We might respond that we are all in favor of getting food to the poor, but public support is lacking and the logistics are complicated. Jesus might point out that we are able to get public support for all sorts of roadways and airports to keep business humming along. So, how hard can it be to sell people on the idea of food for the poor? There are over 100 million Christians in the country and many million more people of goodwill. Jesus might point out that we are able to work out the complicated logistics of building skyscrapers and hosting the Olympics. So, how complicated can it be to get food to everyone in the country? Jesus is suggesting that we move a little faster on these things, that we show a little initiative and imagination.

Then Jesus might wonder why we are not providing more financial support to agencies that serve the poor throughout the world. We might say that we would like to make some donations, but it is so hard to know which agencies are any good. Jesus might respond that clever people with money to invest are able to figure out which companies are any good, which companies will make them some money. They study and do research and spend some time on it. They figure out what to do with their money. Jesus might say we could learn something from those folks.

And then Jesus might wonder what has happened to the gospel message these days. People seem to be losing their enthusiasm, and lots of young people have never been enthusiastic in the first place. We respond that religious services are boring, preachers drone on and on, and we are not quite sure what they are trying to say. No wonder people are losing enthusiasm. We argue that it is hard to reach young people; they are so into their smartphones and video games that getting their attention is a real challenge.

Jesus might respond, "Try harder! It's important." He might recommend that boring, confusing preachers go back to school and learn how to be informative and interesting. If that does not work, perhaps those who are poor public speakers should find some other job to do. Jesus might point out that the owners of Harrah's hotel in Las Vegas would not continue to put Donny Osmond on stage if people found him boring. No, they would call him aside and say, "You'd better freshen up the act a little bit or we are going to hire Lady Gaga."

Jesus might point out that leaders of Starbucks did not waste time wringing their hands over the fact that many people were not drinking coffee anymore. They designed a stylish coffee cup and added chocolate, caramel, and whipped cream to their concoctions to make the coffee more palatable. Now people are buying Starbucks like there is no tomorrow. Jesus might suggest that if religious education directors, teachers, parents, and marketing professionals put their heads together, they could find some way to get young people at least a little bit enthusiastic about the gospel. It is, after all, the greatest news humankind has ever heard!

The gospel story is a challenge to us collectively; it is also a challenge to us individually. Jesus asks, "Are you ambitious enough in the work you do for God's kingdom here on earth?" We might be doing great work as counselors, nurses, judges, parents, and firefighters. But are we ambitious enough? Are we as clever as the politician who spends her days figuring out strategies to advance her career? Are we as dedicated as the athlete who works every day in the weight room, hoping for the big contract that comes with a pro career? Do we take as much initiative as the musician who is looking for that one big break that might make her famous? Are we as ambitious as the devious production supervisor in the gospel story?

We need to hear this story within the wider context of the gospel. The story is intended as a challenge, not as a harsh condemnation. Jesus sees goodness in each one of us, a goodness that does not depend on our hard work or accomplishments. At the same time, Jesus honors us by inviting us to take part in the work of the kingdom of God, a treasure so valuable that wealth, power, and fame pale by comparison. Jesus rejoices in the wonderful work we are already doing and challenges us to be even more ambitious. He invites us to be zealous for that kingdom, to work with great enthusiasm, knowing that we are weak and imperfect and that we can do nothing without God.

I still think the business owner should have locked up the IOUs and not let the production supervisor hang around for two weeks to get into all sorts of monkey business. But that is not the lesson that Jesus intended. Jesus tells us the story of the devious employee to challenge us to be as clever and diligent and to show as much initiative as all the greedy rascals in the world.

Questions to ponder

- *What do you suppose was the production supervisor's primary goal in life? How would you evaluate his strategies for achieving that goal?*

- *Describe a lesson that those of us who are zealous for the kingdom of God might learn from a business that is zealous for profits.*

- *How would you suggest that we generate some enthusiasm for the kingdom of God among young people?*

PART 4

Adventures in Gentile Territory

13
THE TABLE SCRAPS EXCEPTION
Matthew 15:21–28

After concluding their visit in Gennesaret, Jesus and his disciples traveled to Tyre, north of Galilee in Canaanite territory. A trip to the bustling seaport would provide an enjoyable respite.

The group found a large market in the center of town that was crowded with vendors offering a wide variety of exotic items. As they were exploring, a woman hurried to Jesus and asked him to heal her daughter, who was possessed by a demon. Jesus was caught off guard by the unexpected request. The disciples tried to send the woman away, but she only became more insistent. Jesus felt sympathy for the woman but explained that he could not help her. His mission was to the people of Israel; he could not possibly respond to the needs of Canaanites, too. The woman fell to her knees and pleaded for help.

Jesus replied succinctly, "It is not right to take the food of the children and throw it to the dogs."

That is a curious analogy! Jesus' response to the poor woman does not sound very nice. Perhaps the comparison did not seem as harsh in first-century Phoenicia as it does today. Some expressions are difficult to translate. Today in the United States, a business manager might say that supervising her employees is like herding cats. In another culture, people might regard that as a harsh assessment, whereas many of us would consider it a compliment, suggesting that the employees are independent. Jesus' comment about the dogs might be similar: a harmless comparison that gets lost in translation.

The other possibility is that Jesus simply made a mistake. The analogy illustrates Jesus' point well, but perhaps it did not come out quite the way he intended. Maybe, after that, Jesus found a different way of making the same point without the dog comparison. Jesus was human, after all; he did make mistakes.

In any case, Jesus meant no harm, and if we focus all our attention on the analogy, we will miss the main point. Jesus was simply trying to say that he did not have time to attend to the needs of everyone and that he was focusing his attention on the people of Israel. It was not that the rest of the world was unimportant. In fact, Jesus later commissioned his followers to make disciples of all nations. But Jesus simply did not have time to visit all the nations himself. So, he focused his attention on God's chosen people who would serve as a foundation on which the rest of the Church would be built.

Of course, Jesus did not have time to attend to everyone in Israel either. A few months earlier, just outside Capernaum, the disciples told Jesus that everyone was looking for him. Jesus did not return to the city. He needed to get to other towns and was confident that God would watch over the people he left behind. One of the reasons that Jesus recruited disciples and sent them out two by two was that he did not have time to get to all the towns and villages himself.

Jesus had to face his own limitations, like all middle-aged people do.

Knowing all of this might help us understand Jesus better. We can better appreciate his disappointment when he had to turn people away, his frustration when the disciples were slow to learn their lessons, and his distress when he was arrested in Jerusalem.

At the same time, perhaps we can better appreciate the importance of the things on which Jesus chose to spend his time. For example, Jesus spent thirty years with his family, living and working in his hometown, preparing for his public ministry. Thirty precious years in Nazareth. Family, hard work, and preparation for future endeavors were worth it to him.

Once he began his public ministry, Jesus always made time for prayer, frequently sneaking away in the morning. Time was short and the needs were great, but Jesus always made prayer a priority. Jesus also took time for friends, including the disciples, Martha and Mary, the happy couple who got married in Cana, and lots of new friends, too. Friendship was that important. Finally, Jesus took time to share meals frequently with friends and followers, a practice remembered and emulated in the early Church.

All of us who are rushing around as the clocks of our lives are ticking down might take note of Jesus' example. We are encouraged to acknowledge our own limitations, accept the fact that we cannot do everything, and carefully choose the things that we *will* do.

Jesus realized that he could not possibly respond to every request and explained that to the Canaanite woman with his image of children and dogs. However, the woman would not be easily dissuaded. She quickly retorted that even the dogs get the scraps that fall from the family table.

This woman of faith provides another valuable lesson for us. We might call it the "table scraps exception." The exception goes something like this: "Although we need to choose a primary focus to our life and work, we can usually find a few scraps for someone who does not quite fit with the plan."

Apparently, this had not occurred to Jesus before. The Canaanite woman provided Jesus with a valuable insight. Give Jesus credit: unlike most Jewish men of his day, Jesus was able to appreciate the insight of a woman and a foreigner. Jesus complimented the woman on her strong faith and wonderful insight and told her that her daughter would be healed just as she requested.

All of us would do well to be open to new insights from such unexpected sources and to follow the "table scraps exception." Most of our time and energy will be devoted to our families or to those for whom and with whom we work. At the same time, we want to remain open to others with whom we might be able to share a few scraps of our time or talent.

One final lesson from this gospel passage is that we should be persistent in prayer. The poor Canaanite woman was turned down by Jesus not once but twice! But she did not give up; she kept asking and arguing. That does not mean that all our persistent prayers will be answered in the way we would like, but it is important to ask just the same.

This story is packed with lots of little lessons. I suppose that is why Saint Matthew included it in his gospel, curious dog analogy and all.

Questions to ponder

■ *Why do you think the disciples stepped in and tried to send the Canaanite woman away?*

■ *Describe a time when you were forced to turn down a request because you needed to take some time for rest and relaxation.*

■ *Why do you suppose Jesus invites us to be persistent in prayer?*

14
A GIFT OF CRACKLE, WHISTLE, AND BUZZ
Mark 7:31–37

When I first started teaching, I became worried that I had a hearing problem. Students in the classroom would say something and I could not hear it. I needed to move closer and have them repeat what they said. I thought that my hearing might have diminished, unnoticed, during four quiet years of graduate study. I came to realize how important hearing is. Interaction with someone is difficult when you cannot hear what they are saying. My doctor recommended an audiologist, and I had my hearing tested. It turned out that my hearing was fine. Apparently, a number of my students had a voice modulation problem, which, with practice and encouragement, they were able to correct. Interaction in the classroom improved.

On his return from Tyre, Jesus entered the region of the Decapolis and encountered a man who could neither hear nor speak clearly. As the man approached Jesus, he was accompanied by several friends who asked for Jesus' help on the man's behalf.

Obviously, the man had missed out on some wonderful experiences of life. He had not enjoyed music and song or heard the crackle of a fire or the whistle of the wind through the trees. Laughter, rhyme, and the buzz of a crowd anxious in anticipation were lacking from his life. He had missed all the great sounds that we are privileged to enjoy; his life was lived in silence.

Perhaps the greatest hardship of all was losing a connection with those around him. The man found it difficult to communicate with his neighbors and friends. He could not speak clearly to them and could not hear what they said. He not only missed the words but also lost all the nuance contained in tone and volume. He could not enjoy a quiet conversation with a friend, be inspired by a rousing speech, or join his voice with the community in prayer. The man from the Decapolis had lost many connections.

All of us, at one time or another, have hearing and speaking difficulties. These are not the type of problems an audiologist could detect or a speech therapist could correct, but they are problems nonetheless. There are certain voices that we have a hard time hearing, certain words we find difficult to say, certain people with whom we lose connection.

We might have trouble hearing those whose opinions are different from our own. Sorting through difficult questions and considering alternative perspectives require a great deal of work. We like to make judgments quickly and move on. Holding a question open and acknowledging viewpoints that challenge our own are difficult. It is easier to stick with like-minded allies and dismiss those who see things differently. Hearing can be a challenge for us individually and as a country. Polarization seems prevalent these days over issues like crime, health care, and immigration. Part of the problem is that we do not hear each other very well. Part of the problem is that we do not speak in a way that can be understood.

We might also have difficulty hearing those whose experiences or interests are different from ours. We might meet some people from Jamaica and discover that we are worlds apart. They do not understand golf, and we do not understand cricket. They never went to college, and we never faced racial discrimination. Their present concerns and their hopes for the future differ from ours. Letting new people into our lives, learning about their experiences, and sharing our own are challenging things to do. We struggle to hear what they say and to be open to change.

In addition, challenges and criticisms are difficult to receive. If someone is confronting us, whether physically or verbally, we put up our defenses. Sometimes, however, a challenge or a criticism comes from a friend who wants to help us. We still have a hard time hearing it. Sometimes the words go in one ear and out the other without making much of an impact. In a similar way, we might have a hard time speaking a word of constructive criticism to someone else. Either the criticism is not very constructive, or we neglect to say anything at all.

Jesus was anxious to help the man from the Decapolis with the hearing and speaking problems. A crowd was beginning to gather in the street, so Jesus gestured for the man to follow him, and they made their way down a narrow passageway to a quiet spot behind a merchant's tent. After they were seated, Jesus put his fingers into the man's ears and said, "Ephphatha!" ("Be opened!"), and the man could hear. Jesus then spit on his fingers and touched the man's tongue, and

the man could speak clearly. Touching ears and tongues is a little awkward, and Jesus certainly could have chosen a different way to heal the man, but I suspect that Jesus wanted to establish a tangible connection with the poor fellow who had been lacking connection for so long.

Jesus wants to make a connection with us, too. He wants to heal and help us so we can hear better and speak more clearly. We might be inclined to decline Jesus' offer and try to correct our hearing and speaking difficulties on our own. That would be unwise. Jesus knows how difficult hearing and speaking can be at times. We cannot always do it on our own, and he wants to help.

Jesus wants to help us enjoy good conversations with friends, all the more meaningful and satisfying because we can be honest with one another. Jesus wants us to be inspired by someone halfway around the world, whose life and experiences are very different from our own but with whom we share some fundamental concerns and hopes. And Jesus wants us to meet with people whose opinions are at odds with ours. He wants us to be able communicate our thoughts and really listen to what others have to say, so we can work together to address important problems that we share. Jesus wants to touch our ears so we can hear and touch our tongues so we can speak clearly.

Questions to ponder

- *What do you notice about the way Jesus interacted with those who sought healing?*

- *What voices are difficult for you to hear?*

- *Describe a time in your own life when friends or family members assisted you in getting the help you needed.*

15
GOD'S LITTLE FIG TREES
Luke 13:6–9

The man from the Decapolis who had just been healed invited Jesus and the disciples to a feast to celebrate. After the meal, as the sun was setting behind the hills to the west, Jesus regaled the group with a story.

A landowner had a magnificent orchard that extended along the hillside on which her home was perched. She would often stroll through the grove in the late afternoon and appreciate all the wonderful trees. One day in late spring, the owner came across a little fig tree that was barren. She called the gardener over and exclaimed, "Look at this silly little fig tree! We planted it three years ago and it's still not producing any fruit. Why waste the nutrients in the ground? We should just chop it down!"

The gardener could not help but smile at the owner's pronouncement. "Madam, you are correct. This is a silly little fig tree! But let's leave it for this year also. I'll turn up the ground around it and give it some more fertilizer. It may bear fruit in the future. If not, we can chop it down then."

Many years ago, I taught in a high school in Kansas City that was filled with little fig trees. Dominic, a sleepy sapling in his third year, had yet to yield much fruit. In my accounting class, he failed to submit three successive assignments, so I invited him to a special after-school study session.

Dominic ignored the invitation and went to football practice instead. I walked down to the practice field and explained Dominic's dereliction to the football coach. "Dominic!" bellowed the coach, "Get over here right now!" The coach gave his second-string left guard an earful, promised him two extra laps to start the next practice, and entrusted him to my care. I can still hear the clack of Dominic's cleats on the asphalt as we headed back to the classroom building. Study

sessions, football practice, and tough love were just some of the ways that the faculty and staff of the school tended to the little fig trees entrusted to our care.

All of us are like fig trees growing in a garden. God loves his little fig trees, watches over us, and is anxious for us to bear fruit. Our lives bear fruit in a variety of ways. Love is one of the finest fruits of our lives: the deep, wonderful, committed love of married couples; the enduring love of families; the fond affection of friends; and the care and concern we show to those in need. The fruit also includes generosity and the service we provide to one another. Patience, forgiveness, and joy are marvelous fruits, too.

God is anxious for a great harvest and anxious for us. God wants our contributions to make a difference so that we might enjoy rich, satisfying, and meaningful lives. God is like the farmer with high hopes for her little fig trees, anxious for them to bear fruit.

Like the landowner in the story, God has plenty of patience. The landowner is frustrated and disappointed that the little tree does not have any fruit on it, but she is not ready to give up yet. Her threat to cut it down is just blowing smoke. She is putting on a little show for the gardener. The gardener seems to know this; he does not want to give up on the tree either.

The gardener recommends, "leave it for this year also," keeping open the possibility of continuing to try even if it takes a little more time.

"It may bear fruit in the future," he suggests. (Maybe not this coming year, but sometime.) "If not, we can cut it down." (Or we can try another round of fertilizer.)

So it is with God. God does not give up on us. Maybe it will take us a few years to get going. If nothing happens after three years, God will pile on some more fertilizer and wait another year. Fertilizers are friends and family who support and encourage us and make us laugh. Nutrients also include things that lift our spirits, like sunshine, warm days, good food, and beautiful music. Fertilizer is a bit of wisdom someone has shared with us along the way or an insight written in a book, passed along from a previous generation. It is a community that shares our faith and our hope and that gathers with us to pray. Fertilizers are God's grace of wisdom, courage, and peace that penetrate our souls and transform us.

We remember God the farmer and all of God's little fig trees. We ask that God continue to watch over those little trees, water them, give them fertilizer, and not give up on them. Someday they will bear fruit.

Questions to ponder

- *If God is the landowner and we are the fig trees in the story, who might the gardener be?*

- *Describe someone you have known who did not blossom until later in life.*

- *What "fertilizers" have been most helpful to you in your growth as a fig tree?*

16

Catching a Glimpse of the Big Picture

Matthew 17:1-8; Genesis 15:1-6

When I was in junior high, I played clarinet in a concert band. A couple of months before any performance, the band director would pass out new pieces of music. He would instruct us to work on our own for a few weeks before we endeavored to put the whole arrangement together. As the eleventh chair in the clarinet section, working on my own was a challenge, because the part I played did not sound like much all by itself. Whole notes, harmonies, and fifteen-measure rests filled my sheet music. When the band got back together, it took some time for all the parts to fall into place. Once that happened, however, and I heard the entire piece of music, I could see the big picture and realized what my part was all about.

Two people with important parts to play in the concert of life were Abraham, the great patriarch of the people of Israel, and Peter, the disciple of Jesus and an important leader in the early Church. Both Abraham and Peter had moments in their lives when they saw the big picture, occasions when things suddenly became clear. They caught a glimpse of God's plans for the world, and they understood their parts in those plans.

Abram, whom God later named Abraham, received an insight on a clear and quiet night around 2000 BC on a hillside in Canaan. Abram was about seventy-five years old. He and his wife, Sarai (later named Sarah), had been enjoying their retirement years in their homeland of Mesopotamia when God directed them to their new home, four hundred miles to the west. On that quiet night in Canaan, God spoke to Abram and told him of his wonderful plan. God intended to form a brand-new nation, a people who would stay close to God and whom God would watch over with special care. This nation would be a blessing for all the people of the world. God had chosen Abram and Sarai to get the whole thing started.

"Look up at the sky and count the stars, if you can," God said. "Just so, shall your descendants be."

Abram was flabbergasted. He did not even realize that God was interested in the world, much less that God had a plan for it. A plan to form an entire nation from scratch was both magnificent and outrageous. The project would take hundreds of years; it was something only God could do. Getting the whole thing started with a couple of senior citizens was especially preposterous.

Abram caught a glimpse of God's plan that evening in Canaan. The vision took his breath away. Abram understood the part that he and Sarai were to play. They were to settle in this new land and start a family, of all things. Abram realized that it was only a small, first step in God's plan, but it was an important one.

Peter caught a glimpse of the big picture on a cool, sunny day on a mountain near the Sea of Galilee. Jesus had invited Peter, James, and John to join him on the mountaintop because he had something important to show them. Peter was taking in the view when, all of a sudden, a bright light shone from behind him. He turned and saw Jesus twenty feet away, standing on an outcropping of stone and shining as bright as the sun. Two men joined Jesus there, enveloped by the light and conversing like long-lost friends. The short fellow with the bushy eyebrows said something about hearing God's voice on Mount Horeb, and Peter realized that he was Elijah the prophet. And the old, leathery guy with staff in hand must have been Moses, who had received the Ten Commandments on a mountaintop. Suddenly, it became clear to Peter.

Peter knew, of course, that God had a plan and that Jesus was an important part of it. But Peter never realized the size and scope of that plan until that day on the mountaintop. Elijah represented all the prophets, and Moses embodied the Jewish law. Peter realized that the whole history of Israel was leading up to this point from Abraham through the judges, kings, and prophets. It was all preparation for the life and work of Jesus, and the history that would follow would be changed forever.

Peter caught a glimpse of the big picture that day, and it took his breath away. Peter understood better the part he was to play. His was to listen and learn and eventually become a leader of God's people. Like Abraham, Peter realized that it was a small but important piece of a much larger plan.

Every now and again, we try to see the big picture, to catch a glimpse of God's great plans for the world. We can get lost in the details of our own little part. We can focus on the whole notes, harmonies, and fifteen-measure rests and lose sight of the bigger picture. So, every once in a while we stop, step back, and reflect. We join Peter up on the mountaintop to catch a glimpse of what the whole musical piece might sound like when it all comes together. Like Abraham and Peter, we understand better the parts we have been asked to play. We take comfort in knowing that God has arranged the entire score. Up on the mountaintop, we catch a glimpse of God's marvelous plan—and it takes our breath away.

Questions to ponder

- *What do you imagine Moses said to Jesus on the mountaintop?*

- *What is one of your contributions to God's great plans for the world?*

- *How do the contributions of others blend with yours to create beautiful music?*

PART 5

Trouble Brewing in Jerusalem

17
TAKING STOCK OF OUR LIVES
Matthew 25:14–30

Every weekend has key moments. On Friday afternoon, we look forward with anticipation and imagine the possibilities. Saturday evening is the time to savor a weekend well underway but far from over. On Sunday night we take stock of the weekend just completed. We look back to see if it was everything we hoped it would be. The weekend is so filled with possibilities that we would hate to waste it.

Did we have any fun? Did we get out of the house? Did we enjoy a little sunshine, fresh air, and exercise? Did we watch a movie or visit a shopping mall or do something to change up the routine? Getting a little work done is also a consideration. We do not want to work the whole time, but the weekend provides an opportunity for taking care of a few chores or getting caught up on homework. Did we do any of that? And, perhaps most important, did we spend any time enjoying the company of family and friends? On Friday afternoon we look forward to a weekend full of possibilities. On Sunday night we take stock.

Jesus invited his listeners gathered in the Temple in Jerusalem to take stock not of how they had spent their weekend but of how they had spent their lives. He told a story about a noble and his three servants.

The noble prepared for a journey and entrusted to the three members of his staff the care of his wealth while he was away. To Amnon, the head of the household, he gave five talents. To Bohan, his property manager, he gave two talents, and to Caleb, the stable hand, he gave one.

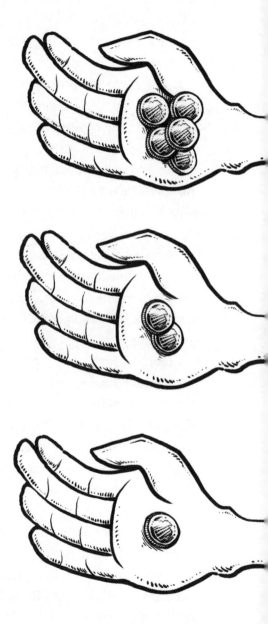

Within a month, Amnon had invested half his money in a very promising brickmaking operation and the other half in an import-export business. Bohan purchased acreage in a fertile valley outside of town and hired workers to plant and manage a vegetable crop. Caleb buried his talent in the barn.

When the noble returned, he called his servants to settle accounts. Amnon stepped forward and announced, "Master, you gave me five talents. I have made five more!"

"Well done!" the master exclaimed. "I will give you even greater responsibilities."

Bohan came forward and said, "Master, with your two talents I have earned two more."

"Excellent!" replied the noble. "You, too, will share in my joy."

Finally, Caleb approached with his eyes down and handed the single talent to his master. "I was worried since you are so demanding, so I buried the talent in the barn for safe keeping. Here it is back."

"You wicked, lazy servant!" the noble shouted. "Could you not have done something with the talent? You could have put it in the bank, at least, to earn a little interest. Throw this man out of here and give his talent to someone who will do something with it!"

I feel bad for Caleb. Apparently, he was not as capable as the other staff members, and the master knew it. I was hoping that he would really come through in the end and prove his master wrong. He did not. Caleb buried the talent, forgot about it, and just gave it back to the master when he returned. The servant was afraid, and we can understand that. Worried about losing it all, he wanted to avoid taking any chances, so he kept the talent hidden. Lack of imagination was another problem. Caleb could not envision what he could do with a talent.

Jesus invites us to imagine ourselves at the end of the world taking stock of our lives. Did we make good use of the gifts we had been given? Gifts include good health, good education, talents, and abilities. Did we bury those in the ground or do something with them?

Of course, investing personal talents, as with financial talents, is a risky proposition. The pursuit of a career or a vocation in life might end in failure. Jesus encourages us, "Do not be afraid. Give it a shot; see what happens. Taking a chance will be well worth it." Some of our undertakings might not succeed, but we will earn a far greater return by investing boldly than by playing it safe our whole life long. Jesus invites us to imagine the possibilities, to dream big dreams.

Jesus wants us to be part of the kingdom of God, to help build a world of justice, compassion, peace, service, and care for those most in need. The kingdom of God is too important to think small. When we get to the end of our life, Jesus wants to be able to look back with us and say, "Well done! You generated a great return on your investment."

Of course, a life, like a weekend, is not all about work. As we look back, we want to be able to say that we had some fun, enjoyed life, appreciated the wonderful gifts God gave us, and grew in our affection for family and friends. It would be a shame to rush through life without ever marveling at a magnificent sunset, delighting in a novel that captures our imagination, or savoring a favorite meal cooked to perfection.

Family and friends are of special importance. Jesus had a very simple, two-part commandment: love God and love one another. That commandment is definitely going to be on the final exam. Did we take the time to grow in love with the people in our lives? Love is a risky proposition, too, of course, but as Saint Paul says, "If we do not have love, why bother?" Jesus says, "Do not be afraid. Love is worth it."

When the end of the world comes, we want to be able to look back on lives filled with family and friends and love shared with all sorts of people.

If life is like a weekend, some are still enjoying Friday night. Jesus invites those with their lives in front of them to dream big dreams and imagine the possibilities for their part in the kingdom of God. Some of the rest of us are well into the Saturday or Sunday of life. Jesus invites us to savor our lives filled with good work, rich relationships, beauty, laughter, and joy. Someday, we will all get to the big Sunday night of life. On that day, may we be able to offer back to God a good return on all the wonderful gifts we have been given.

Questions to ponder

- *Why do you suppose the noble entrusted Caleb with anything? Why did the noble not simply divide the talents between the more trustworthy members of the staff?*

- *What God-given talent have you invested well?*

- *In looking over the past year, what do you wish you had spent more time doing?*

18
FORGIVING THE UNFORGIVABLE
John 8:2–11

As Jesus concluded a parable to a group gathered in the Temple, a clamoring mob approached from the south gate. A Pharisee stepped forward along with two members of the Temple guard holding a woman by either arm. The Pharisee announced that the woman had been caught in the act of adultery and asked Jesus for his opinion on the matter. One of the scribes pointedly reminded everyone that the law of Moses called for stoning.

The aggrieved husband and his two brothers stood behind the Pharisee. Betrayed and disgraced by the woman's infidelity, they were angry and wanted retribution, a suitable punishment for the crime. Exasperated by the delay, one of the brothers shouted, "The Sanhedrin should condemn her now! What are you waiting for?"

Others in the group did not know the woman or her husband but were outraged nonetheless. Infidelity was a threat to any marriage and needed to be prevented with strong deterrents. They wanted a severe sentence to be imposed on the woman and voiced support for a quick judgment.

The religious leaders in the crowd thought that Jesus was too kind to sinners and too lax in his observance of the law. The law had come from God and needed to be followed. It ensured that justice was done and that the community remained in God's good graces. The adultery case would force Jesus to make his position clear, providing an opportunity to damage his credibility and to gather evidence to use against him.

Terrible sins are committed today and elicit the same reactions. Emma, after a tirade of invective against her family, moves away and never calls. She even refuses to attend her father's funeral the following year. Her brothers are hurt and angry and are eager for some sort of payback. Holt is convicted of selling fentanyl and heroin in his hometown in rural Arkansas. It is his first offense, but his neighbors call for a harsh sentence. Drugs are destroying their families and their community, and the neighbors want strong deterrents to discourage other drug dealers. Hector, a college student, spray paints derogatory obscenities about gays and lesbians on the wall of a residence hall. His classmates recognize how hurtful the words are and are anxious to have him expelled. They want the university to stand up for what is right; they want justice.

Jesus did not answer the Pharisee's question but instead bent down and began writing in the sand with his finger. He was not going to get into an argument about the law with the religious leaders. He certainly was not going to allow the accused woman to become a case study. Jesus understood the husband's anger and his neighbors' outrage but did not want them acting on those emotions. He hoped that a little quiet time might allow some of the strong reactions to subside.

Jesus' response to sins committed today is much the same. Laws and rules are important in any society, but the imposition of punishments on offenders can neither undo the harm that was done nor achieve the justice that we seek. Jesus encourages us to respond to sin not out of anger or fear but out of a careful consideration of what is best for both the community and the one who has sinned.

Emma's refusal to attend her father's funeral was hurtful to her family, but retribution solves nothing and indeed makes things worse. Far better would be for her brothers

to seek reconciliation with their estranged sister. Holt will probably do some prison time for his crime; laws are only meaningful if consequences are imposed for violating them. But a harsh sentence for a first offense is unwarranted and will do little to stop the spread of illegal drugs. Holt needs a fresh start after his time in prison, and his community needs to find positive ways to address the drug problem. Hector hurt many people, too, by spray painting slurs on the residence hall walls. Suspension might be the only answer if he remains recalcitrant. But if Hector is contrite and willing to apologize, the university might find ways to help him learn from his mistakes and be reconciled with other students.

Impatient with all the waiting, the Pharisee pressed Jesus for an answer. Jesus stood up and, looking over the group, invited the one without any sin to throw the first stone. He bent down again and traced more letters in the sand.

The Pharisee and the other religious leaders recognized that Jesus had thwarted their attempt to trap him. Rather than arguing about the proper interpretation of the law, he invited the crowd to consider what true justice entails. There was no way for the scholars of the law to win that debate. Exasperated, the Pharisee muttered something under his breath and stormed away. The Temple guard released the woman and headed back to their posts. The husband of the accused woman began to voice an objection, but his brothers encouraged him to give up the fight and move on with his life. The rest of the crowd, after reflecting a bit on their own failings, were not going to press the point. They left, too.

Only the woman remained. Jesus straightened up and asked her if there was anyone left to condemn her. "No one," she answered.

"Neither do I," Jesus said. "You are free to go, but avoid this sin in the future."

Jesus invites us to make reconciliation part of our lives and to share his concern for those who have wandered away. Jesus invites us to make forgiving love the mark of our communities. He encourages us not to abandon those who have made terrible mistakes but to welcome all those who desire to be part of our community. Our communities are weak, broken, and imperfect because all of us, in some way, are weak, broken, and imperfect. Jesus invites us to recognize and accept that reality, to continue to seek and extend forgiveness, and to ask for God's healing and strength.

Questions to ponder

■ *What lessons do you suppose the disciples learned by watching Jesus during this encounter?*

■ *Describe a time when you have seen strong negative emotions toward a wrongdoer hamper a careful consideration of the appropriate response.*

■ *Which sinners are most difficult for members of your civic or religious community to forgive?*

19
A POIGNANT SIGN OF HONOR AND AFFECTION
John 12:1–11; Matthew 26:6–13

A large crowd gathered for dinner at the home of Martha, Mary, and Lazarus. Jesus had made the trip from Jerusalem with a group of his disciples. Several friends and followers from Bethany had also been invited. As Martha and some neighbors were putting the finishing touches on the meal, Mary and Lazarus seated the guests in the courtyard outside their home and offered them something to drink. The visitors enjoyed reconnecting with acquaintances they had not seen in a while. Even so, the mood was subdued. The friends and followers of Jesus were worried about him. Religious leaders in Jerusalem had become more vocal in their opposition to him. Some claimed that Jesus was a charlatan and never actually healed anyone. Powerful people were eager to put a stop to his ministry.

Martha and Mary were worried about their brother, too. Miraculously, Lazarus had been brought back to life by Jesus several months earlier. The chief priests refused to acknowledge it, so intent were they on discrediting Jesus. Lazarus was told explicitly not to speak of Jesus again and to stop claiming that a miraculous healing had taken place. The party that evening would undoubtedly draw more unwanted attention to Lazarus. Nevertheless, the sisters had decided not to let their worries get in the way of the celebration.

The meal was marvelous. Roasted lamb seasoned with flavorful herbs was served with an assortment of steamed vegetables and freshly baked bread. A rich red wine complemented the meal. As serving platters were passed and the wine was poured, the conversation became more animated. The guests were able to forget about their concerns for a while. Jesus recounted adventures from his recent travels and encouraged his disciples to share stories of their own.

Matthew and John did their best to join in the conversation but were troubled by the menacing opposition in Jerusalem. They remained quiet and downcast for much of the meal. Lazarus made a point of connecting with each of them during the course of the evening to offer words of encouragement and support.

The trouble brewing in Jerusalem was obvious to the friends of Jesus. It was obvious to Jesus, too. He recognized that opposition had been growing for some time. The authority he claimed through his instruction and wondrous miracles threatened the authority of the religious establishment. Jesus' invitations to mercy, forgiveness, and care for those on the edges of society undercut the Pharisees' insistence on strict observance of the law. And, of course, Jesus' criticisms of the behavior of religious leaders only made them angrier. Jesus recognized the opposition, but he remained faithful to what God called him to do and say.

Jesus raised Lazarus from the dead as a powerful sign of God's love and power, knowing that it would only intensify the opposition. Jesus returned to Jerusalem a short time later, aware of the hostility he would face. He visited Bethany one last time because he very much wanted to be there for his friends.

After Mary helped clear the dishes, she went back into the house to retrieve a jar of perfumed oil that she had purchased from a street vendor in Jerusalem a week earlier. Mary spent a sizeable portion of her savings on the special mixture of oil, myrrh, and spices, but it was a purchase that she very much wanted to make. She was anxious to show Jesus a small sign of honor, fidelity, and love.

As Mary stepped out to the courtyard with the jar of oil, conversations died down, and the guests turned their attention to her. Mary approached Jesus and asked to anoint his head. Jesus, filled with affection for his friend, agreed without hesitation. He bowed his head and Mary slowly poured the perfumed oil, which filled the air with its fragrance as it flowed through Jesus' hair and down his beard. As the guests watched in silence, Mary's eyes filled with tears.

Mary was sad because of the way that the whole world had failed Jesus. This holy man, whose life was filled with compassion, generosity, and hope, was now subject to hostility and ridicule. His very life was threatened. Mary anointed Jesus in anticipation of his burial, recognizing how precarious his life was.

Mary was stirred not only by sadness but also by love. Jesus was her teacher, her Lord, and her dear friend. She wanted to extend a small kindness to show him how much he meant to her. On behalf of his followers, Mary anointed

Jesus as their king. She wanted him to know that many still believed in him.

Suddenly, Judas broke the silence. "Why was money spent on this extravagant oil?" he asked, his voice filled with incredulity. "The money could have been given to the poor!"

The crowd was stunned. "Judas, don't ...," Peter implored.

"Leave her alone," Jesus added. "Why do you criticize Mary's beautiful gesture? You can give money to the poor anytime you like."

Jesus took Mary's trembling hands in his own. Looking into her eyes, he said softly, "Thank you."

Mary is a model of love. We hope to become more like her. As we grow in love for Jesus, we share her sadness that we have failed him both individually and collectively. We mourn the fact that he faced so much hatred and ridicule. Like Mary, we wish to show Jesus a sign of our high regard for him. Unable to invite him to dinner or anoint him with oil, we honor Jesus by living well the life to which he has

called us and show our love for him by caring for the people in our lives.

Questions to ponder

- *What do you imagine was Jesus' reaction to the dinner in Bethany?*

- *What do you imagine is Jesus' reaction to the goodness and love in your life?*

- *How would you honor a friend or family member for whom you have high regard?*

20
¡Viva Cristo Rey!

Luke 20:20–26;

23:1–4, 13–24, 32–38

Jesus exhorted a large crowd gathered near one of the Temple porticos to greater faithfulness to God. As he paused, preparing to move to a new topic, a Pharisee interjected, "Is it allowed for us to pay a tax to Caesar?"

Jesus looked at the man and asked, "Whose image and whose inscription is on the coin you would use to pay such a tax?"

"Caesar's," came the response.

"Then give to Caesar what is Caesar's but give to God what is God's," Jesus concluded.

The religious leader was trying to trap Jesus. His question suggested that the kingdom of God that Jesus announced was at odds with the Roman Empire. If the Pharisees could provoke Jesus into publicly opposing Roman rule, the Sanhedrin could bring a charge of insurrection against him.

Jesus did not take the bait. The kingdom of God is not an earthly realm competing against others for power, land, and wealth. Membership in the kingdom of God does not exclude membership in earthly nations and the practical obligations such membership entails. At the same time, our lives and all of creation belong to God, and we engage in the affairs of the world guided by that understanding.

In 1925, Pope Pius XI reminded Christians that our lives are dedicated to God by establishing the Feast of Christ the King. In a time of strong nationalism, the reminder was opportune. The pope invited all the faithful to continue to testify, in both word and action, to their obedience and allegiance to Christ.

Miguel Pro was a Jesuit priest who lived and worked in Mexico in the 1920s. A revolution had just ended, and a new constitution had been adopted that attempted to limit the power and influence of the Catholic Church. Among other things, celebrating Mass was illegal. Miguel Pro ignored that law; he was going to continue to celebrate the Eucharist no matter what the government said. He traveled around Mexico City and the surrounding area, offering Mass for small communities that would gather in secret. He had a wonderful sense of humor and wore all kinds of disguises to avoid detection. Eventually, the authorities caught up with him. They convicted him on unsubstantiated charges and executed him by firing squad in a plaza outside the city jail. As he faced his executioners, Miguel Pro spread his arms and said a simple prayer, "¡Viva Cristo Rey!" Long live Christ the King!

We might reflect on the impact our allegiance to Christ the King has in our own lives. Some Christians live in nations where they are prohibited from praying to God, instructing others in the faith, or defending the rights of the poor and the oppressed. Many courageously remain faithful to God in the face of the same dangers that Miguel Pro faced.

Many of us are fortunate to live in countries that allow the free practice of the faith. For the most part, we are able to live the lives of compassion, prayer, and service to which God calls us. We work with a wide variety of people to address shared concerns. We try to help our nations and our leaders become more just, merciful, and responsive to the needs of the poor and the powerless.

At the same time, following Jesus sometimes brings us into conflict with our countries and our leaders. We might be called to protest laws or policies and seek to change them. We might be called to violate laws that we consider unjust and risk arrest. Our fidelity to Christ the King sometimes means being at odds with the government.

Even as we have high hopes for our government and hold it to high standards, we realize that political solutions, in themselves, are never enough. We do not want our hopes for the kingdom of God limited by what government can do. Legislation can respond to the needs of the poor and reduce violence and discrimination. But laws are not enough. We need generous, loving, and compassionate hearts. The small, quiet steps we take toward building the kingdom in our corner of the world are just as important as big national initiatives.

Soon after his exchange with the Pharisee about Roman taxes, Jesus was arrested by the Temple guard under cover of darkness. Jesus' teaching threatened the authority of the religious leaders, and they wanted to put a stop to it. In the house of the chief priest, the Sanhedrin charged and convicted Jesus of blasphemy. The following morning, members of the Sanhedrin brought him to the procurator's compound, seeking a penalty of death. They informed Pilate that Jesus claimed to be king and falsely accused him of forbidding the payment of taxes to Caesar. Pilate thought the charge brought against the scruffy country preacher was absurd, but he asked anyway, "Are you the King of the Jews?"

Jesus recognized that he could not provide a satisfactory answer and simply acknowledged the question.

Pilate intended to have Jesus scourged and released, but the religious leaders incited the crowd to demand crucifixion. Pilate ordered Jesus' execution as a matter of expediency. He had a sign posted on the cross on which Jesus hung that read "King of the Jews" to memorialize the accusation against him. Without realizing it, Pilate was also acknowledging the kingship of Jesus that his followers have proclaimed ever since. ¡Viva Cristo Rey!

Questions to ponder

- *Why do you suppose that people who supported Jesus earlier in the week turned against him on Good Friday?*

- *Have you ever experienced a time when following Jesus brought you into conflict with what civil law required? If so, describe what happened.*

- *Describe a national initiative that Jesus and his followers would likely support.*

PART 6

Love Stronger Than Death

21
Rescued from the Stormy Waters

John 1:1–5, 14; 11:25–26; 20:11–18

Life is like a sunny, summer day on a vast, shimmering beach. The beach stretches in either direction as far as the eye can see. White sand, palm trees, and clear blue water. We have everything we need for a day in the sun: colorful

umbrellas, volleyball nets, barbecue grills, and coolers full of cold beverages.

God says, "Enjoy yourselves. Just be careful. Don't go out too far in the water. The surf can get choppy out there. And be sure to come back to shore when it gets dark. Storms can blow through at night."

Unfortunately, humans are stubborn, foolish, and inattentive. No sooner does God remind us to be careful than we start playing in the deep water, get caught in an undertow, and are pulled far away from shore. The water is rough, and we can hardly hold on to our inflatable swim tube. We start paddling around but are not even sure which direction we should go. Then the wind picks up, the rain starts falling, the sky darkens, and we are in serious trouble.

We always seem to get ourselves into a terrible mess. It has been that way throughout history. The wind, the waves, and the storm are the constant conflicts and divisions, the hatred and the fear, the greed and the malice. We get caught in the middle of those storms and we can find no way out. Add to that the darkness of sickness and death and we do not stand a chance.

The remarkable thing is that God still loves us. You would think that God would have given up on us long ago. But, no, God loves us. God stands on the shore as the sky turns dark and the clouds roll in. God stares out to the ocean and worries about us. Throughout history, God has tried to help us find our way back. God turns on a big spotlight and sweeps it across the dark waters, hoping we might see it. God sounds a loud foghorn, hoping it might guide us back. But nothing seems to work; we are no match for the wind and the waves;

hatred, greed, and fear have too much power over us. So, God decided to do an amazing thing. God sent his Son into the stormy waters to try to find us and bring us back.

Jesus shared our human life. He enjoyed and appreciated the wonder and joy of the sunny days and sparkling beaches that are part of human life. Jesus also joined us out in the ocean, far from shore, and witnessed firsthand the dangers of greed, fear, and sickness. During his last few days on earth, Jesus faced a terrible storm in Jerusalem. He encountered hatred, jealousy, deception, betrayal, and violence. But the storm is not the end of the story.

During the quiet early morning hours of Easter Sunday, God raised Jesus from the dead. The storm clouds cleared, the sun came out, and Jesus made it back to shore. More than that, Jesus found us and brought us back, too. We are shivering and coughing up water, and we lost our inflatable swim tube, but Jesus saved us and gave us life again.

As time goes on, we appreciate more the wonder and the power of God's love because we know how powerful and deadly the storm can be.

Wars and armed conflicts plague the Middle East, Eastern Europe, Sub-Saharan Africa, and other regions of the world. Explosions and gunfire erupt with regularity. Thousands of precious lives are lost as hatred and violence grow.

Callousness and greed infect the business world. Stockholders demand a higher return, so companies demand more profits, so suppliers demand lower costs. All these demands create low wages and terrible working conditions halfway around the world. Greed and injustice continue to have a devastating impact on people's lives.

Friends and family members battle cancer and other ailments. We have learned far too much about a variety of illnesses and their treatments—more than we ever wanted to know. Sickness and death provide regular reminders of human frailty.

The wind, waves, and storms are still around; darkness rolls in on a regular basis, and people continue to make bad choices. But the story does not end there; Easter happened, and Easter changes everything. No matter how dark the skies or how fierce the storm, Jesus is with us through it all. He will quiet the winds in wondrous ways if we allow him to do so. He will shine a light in the darkness to show us the way. He will even rescue us from our own foolishness. If we just keep holding on to him, we will have life right now, just like God planned it, and life in the kingdom yet to come, because God's love is that strong.

We remember that God's love is stronger than all the hatred and fear in the world, that God's generosity is more powerful than greed, and that God's life overcomes poverty, sickness, and even death. We celebrate the day when the storm clouds cleared, the sun came out, and Jesus made it back to shore with us.

Questions to ponder

- *Recount a gospel story that shows Jesus choosing to swim out into the stormy waters of life.*

- *How has your faith provided light during dark, difficult days?*

- *Describe an institution formed by people of faith that has brought love and life to stormy waters in the world.*

22

Cleopas and What's-his-name

Luke 24:13–33

"The high priest got him killed," Cleopas argued as he and a traveling companion trudged north from Jerusalem. "If it wasn't for him, Jesus would still be alive and would have a huge crowd of supporters."

"And then what?" the companion asked. "The Romans would have put a stop to it sooner or later. We were foolish to think that a holy man could ever withstand the force of the Roman Empire."

Cleopas and his buddy had joined Jesus' company a few months earlier, convinced that he was going to become a great leader of Israel by acclamation of the people. They hoped that under his leadership, Israel would one day claim its rightful sovereignty, shaking free from the control of the Roman Empire. But then Jesus was arrested, charged with sedition, and crucified. Their hopes vanished in an instant. Once the Sabbath was over, Cleopas and his friend packed their bags, said goodbye to the other disciples, and headed for home.

"What are you arguing about?" came a voice from behind. The two travelers turned to see a stranger quickly approaching.

"Are you the only visitor to Jerusalem who did not hear the news?" Cleopas asked. Then he proceeded to explain the events of the past few days. As they walked along, the stranger explained how Scripture shed light on all these events. Cleopas and his companion had no idea to whom they were talking.

The fact that the two disciples did not recognize Jesus is one of the striking things about this little episode. For months they had gathered with the crowds to listen to Jesus speak and were struck by his words. They had seen him perform miracles and were convinced that he had come from God. They had put their hope in him. Just a few days earlier, they had seen Jesus teaching in the Temple. Now he was walking right beside them, sharing insights from Scripture, and they did not even realize it. They did not yet have the eyes of faith to see.

Belief and hope in the resurrection require faith. Jesus appeared only to those who had faith. Our relationship with Jesus and our hope in the resurrection require a leap of faith. We cannot prove the resurrection scientifically. We cannot convince someone of the resurrection through logical argument alone. A leap of faith is required.

Another striking thing about the story is that we know the name of only one of the travelers: Cleopas. The other person is anonymous. This imbalance is one of the reasons that scholars are convinced that Luke was not the first one to tell this story. If this were a Lucan original, he would have included both names. It is much more likely that this story had been passed along for forty or fifty years before Luke included it in his gospel. By that time, no one could remember the name of the other fellow in the story. I picture Cleopas and old what's-his-name up in heaven having a good laugh every time this story is retold, with Cleopas giving his buddy a hard time that the storytellers forgot his name.

Having old what's-his-name included in the story is a good reminder that, after the resurrection, Jesus appeared to some rather ordinary folks, people who were not movers and shakers, people who were not famous. Just as important, the story reminds us that Jesus continues to walk with all sorts of his followers, most of whom are mostly anonymous, like us.

A common mistake is to think that the kingdom of God happens only in extraordinary places among extraordinary people. Yes, the kingdom of God is growing in a refugee camp in Thailand as relief workers provide food and medical care to people in desperate need. Yes, the kingdom of God is at work in south-central Los Angeles as police and government officials try to arrange a peace settlement between gangs. Yes, the kingdom of God is growing among a group of cloistered nuns in an abbey in the middle of nowhere. But the kingdom of God is growing in lots of ordinary places, too. It is growing wherever followers of Jesus are responding to his invitation to love, reconciliation, and service. Jesus is right there with them.

As the three travelers neared the village of Emmaus, Cleopas invited the friendly stranger to stop for the night with them. They were happy to discover that the local inn had room and had not yet put away the evening meal. After they had stashed their traveling gear and were comfortably seated in the dining area, the innkeeper's daughter brought them bowls of hot soup and a platter of bread. The stranger offered a blessing and then broke the bread and began passing it around. Suddenly, Cleopas and his buddy realized that their dinner companion was Jesus. At that same instant Jesus disappeared from sight.

Jesus had joined Cleopas and what's-his-name on the journey because they were his followers and friends. He was interested in their lives, needed their help, and wanted to support and encourage them. Jesus shows up in our lives, too, for the same reasons. Of course, followers today do not always recognize his presence either.

Jesus is in the kitchen with a fellow who is fixing dinner for his family. The fellow is chopping onions and celery and talking to his daughter about the latest much-anticipated Pixar movie. Why is Jesus in the kitchen? Jesus is there because he loves the little girl and her dad and is interested in their lives. Jesus visits families because families are terrific and because family life is one of the best ways for us to love one another.

Jesus is sitting at a production department meeting around a crowded table covered with notepads, laptops, and coffee cups. Jesus does not have a great affection for meetings, but he is with the production department that morning because work is holy and provides a way for us to serve one another. Jesus realizes that meetings are important. At meetings, some key decisions get made that will have a real impact on people's lives. Jesus attends the meeting because he is interested in what happens.

Jesus is along for a late-night Chipotle run with friends. Jesus hops in the car because he hates to miss a good meal and likes burritos. But mostly Jesus is there because of the friendship shared that night. He is very interested in friendship and wants to be part of it.

These are not earth-shattering events, but that is the point. The kingdom of God gets played out in all sorts of places in very ordinary ways. Jesus wants to be a part of all of them.

Sometimes, we fail to realize that Jesus is walking along the road of life with us. To help us remember, we do the same thing that Cleopas and what's-his-name did. We gather around a table as friends and fellow travelers to share a simple meal. As we break the bread and pass it around, we realize that Jesus is right there with us and has been with us all along.

Questions to ponder

- *How did the faith of Cleopas and his buddy grow as they walked along the road with Jesus?*

- *Describe an event or interaction that happened in your life this past month during which Jesus was very likely present.*

- *What part of the celebration of the Eucharist or other religious service is most helpful to you in recognizing the presence of Jesus?*

SELECT BIBLIOGRAPHY

Brown, Raymond E., SS, Joseph A. Fitzmyer, SJ, and Roland E. Murphy, OCarm, eds. *The New Jerome Biblical Commentary*. Englewood Cliffs: Prentice Hall, 1990.

Castelot, John J., and Aelred Cody, OSB. "Religious Institutions of Israel." In Brown et al., *The New Jerome Biblical Commentary*, 1253–83.

Clifford, Richard J., SJ. "Exodus." In Brown et al., *The New Jerome Biblical Commentary*, 44–60.

———— and Roland E. Murphy, OCarm. "Genesis." In Brown et al., *The New Jerome Biblical Commentary*, 8–43.

Dillon, Richard J. "Acts of the Apostles." In Brown et al., *The New Jerome Biblical Commentary*, 722–67.

Donahue, John R., SJ, and Daniel J. Harrington. *The Gospel of Mark*. Sacra Pagina Series. Vol. 2. Collegeville: Liturgical Press, 2002.

Gench, Frances Taylor. *Back to the Well: Women's Encounters with Jesus in the Gospels*. Louisville: Westminster John Knox Press, 2004.

Ghezzi, Bert. *Voices of the Saints: A 365-Day Journey with Our Spiritual Companions*. Chicago: Loyola Press, 2009.

Harrington, Daniel J., SJ. "The Gospel According to Mark." In Brown et al., *The New Jerome Biblical Commentary*, 596–629.

————. *The Gospel of Matthew*. Sacra Pagina Series. Vol. 1. Collegeville: Liturgical Press, 2007.

Johnson, Luke Timothy. *The Gospel of Luke*. Sacra Pagina Series. Vol. 3. Collegeville: Liturgical Press, 1991.

Karris, Robert J., OFM. "The Gospel According to Luke." In Brown et al., *The New Jerome Biblical Commentary*, 675–721.

King, Philip J., and Lawrence E. Stager. *Life in Biblical Israel*. Louisville: John Knox Press, 2001.

Laffey, Alice L. "Ruth." In Brown et al., *The New Jerome Biblical Commentary*, 553–57.

Lumen Gentium: Dogmatic Constitution on the Church. Second Vatican Council. Promulgated by Pope Paul VI. November 21, 1964.

Meier, John P. "Jesus." In Brown et al., *The New Jerome Biblical Commentary*, 1316–28.

Moloney, Francis J., SDB. *The Gospel of John*. Sacra Pagina Series. Vol. 4. Collegeville: Liturgical Press, 1998.

Murphy-O'Connor, Jerome, OP. "The First Letter to the Corinthians." In Brown et al., *The New Jerome Biblical Commentary*, 798–815.

Perkins, Pheme. "The Gospel According to John." In Brown et al., *The New Jerome Biblical Commentary*, 942–85.

Pius XI. *Quas Primas*. The Holy See, December 11, 1925, www.vatican.va/content/pius-xi/en/encyclicals/documents/hf_p-xi_enc_11121925_quas-primas.html.

Puhl, Louis J., SJ. *The Spiritual Exercises of St. Ignatius, Based on Studies in the Language of the Autograph*. Chicago: Loyola, 1951.

Tylenda, Joseph N., SJ. *A Pilgrim's Journey: The Autobiography of Ignatius of Loyola*. Wilmington: Michael Glazier, 1985.

Viviano, Benedict T., OP. "The Gospel According to Matthew." In Brown et al., *The New Jerome Biblical Commentary*, 630–74.

Walsh, Jerome T., and Christopher T. Begg. "1–2 Kings." In Brown et al., *The New Jerome Biblical Commentary*, 160–85.

Wright, Addison G., SS, Roland E. Murphy, OCarm, and Joseph A. Fitzmyer, SJ. "A History of Israel." In Brown et al., *The New Jerome Biblical Commentary*, 1219–52.